Slow Food Nation's
Come to the Table

Slow Food Nation's
Come to the Table

The Slow Food Way of Living

Edited by **KATRINA HERON**
Foreword by **ALICE WATERS**

Rodale books may be purchased for business or promotional use or for special sales. For information, please write to:

Special Markets Department, Rodale Inc., 733 Third Avenue, New York, NY 10017

Printed in the United States of America

Rodale Inc. makes every effort to use acid-free ⊗, recycled paper ♻.

Book design by David Albertson Design

Photos were provided by the following:
Aya Brackett: cover photograph
Jenny Elia Pfeiffer: pages ii, vi, viii, xi, xii; xvi–1, 156; all photos of Full Belly Farm, Burroughs Family Farms, Will Scott Jr.,
Windborne Farm, Vang and Moua Family Farms, and J&P Organics; and all recipe photos, with the exception of page 109
Emily Nathan: pages 106–107, 109, and all photos of Sweet Home Ranch
Kim Westerman: all photos of Clark Summit Farm, Pixie Growers, and Redwood Roots Farm
Alexander Stock: all photos of Tamai Family Farm
Robert Farmer: page 102 *(top row, right)*
Beth Ann Levendoski: page 102 *(top row, left and middle; middle row, left and right)*
Leah Davida: page 102 *(middle row, middle; bottom row, right)*
Beth Ann Levendoski: page 102 *(top row, left and middle; middle row, left and right; bottom row, left)*

Library of Congress Cataloging-in-Publication Data

Slow food nation's come to the table / edited by Katrina Heron with forward by Alice Waters.
    p.   cm.
Includes index.
ISBN-13 978–1–60529–895–5 hardcover
ISBN-10 1–60529–895–6 hardcover
    1. Cookery (Natural foods)   2. Slow food movement—California.   I. Heron, Katrina.   II. Waters, Alice.
TX741.S586 2008
641.5'636—dc22   2008030251

Distributed to the trade by Macmillan

2   4   6   8   10   9   7   5   3   1 hardcover

We inspire and enable people to improve their lives and the world around them
For more of our products visit **rodalestore.com** or call 800-848-4735

slow food \slō füd\ *n. See also:* REAL FOOD. **1 :** An alternative to "fast food." **2 :** A descriptive phrase for food that can be traced to its source, esp. food that is produced without chemical and/or other industrial processes. **3 :** A celebration of food traditions, emphasizing seasonal and regional qualities. **4 :** A description of the fundamental human activity of preparing, eating, enjoying, and sharing healthy, flavorful food. **5 :** A global food initiative seeking to counter the industrialized food system's environmentally and culturally unsustainable methods and their consequences. **6 :** A relationship with food that centers on the values of "good, clean, and fair": healthy and delicious ingredients, produced with ecologically sound and humane methods, on a fair economic model. **7 :** Any delicious snack or meal, simple or elaborate, from real ingredients. **8 :** Read on . . .

Contents

COMING BACK TO EARTH ix

Farm Stories xvi

Full Belly Farm 3

Sweet Home Ranch 13

Tamai Family Farms 23

Burroughs Family Farms 29

Will Scott Jr. 41

Windborne Farm 49

Clark Summit Farm 59

Vang and Moua Family Farms... 67

Pixie Growers 79

J&P Organics 85

Redwood Roots Farm 93

Tierra Miguel Farm 103

Recipes.. 106

HOW TO GO SLOW 154

ABOUT SLOW FOOD 157

INDEX 158

CONTRIBUTORS 160

Coming Back to Earth

Vandana Shiva, the outspoken Indian food activist, has said that farms are zones of peace on this planet. I believe it. Both farms and gardens teach us the cycles of nature—ways to replenish the soil, the natural role of bugs and worms, the importance of planting according to the seasons, how things grow and ripen, and when it's time to harvest. Gardens also teach us that the healthiest foods on earth—the fresh fruits and vegetables we all know we're supposed to eat—are actually the most delicious, as long as they're raised right, prepared simply, and eaten when ripe.

There is no better place than the farmers' market to find the best produce of the season, and more and more of us are getting in the spirit by growing a few things ourselves on a spare garden patch. (I especially love the radishes, lettuces and herbs right outside my window.) When people ask me how to get started cooking with fresh, seasonal ingredients, I tell them, always explore your garden and go to the market before you decide what to cook. Plan your menu around what you find there. Select produce that looks freshly harvested and at its peak—food that looks *alive*. You know a lot more about the look and feel and smell and taste of real food than you may think. I've always thought the freshness of food should speak for itself! And if you've just discovered a new vegetable or fruit, the way to find out how best to prepare it is to learn from the farmer who grew it.

As we were composing this book, I went down to Fresno to visit an old friend, Mas Masumoto. Mas grew up on the farm where he and his family—his wife, Marcy, and their two children, Nikiko and Korio—now grow peaches,

Alice Waters and Mas Masumoto having breakfast at the farm.

nectarines, and grapes. Mas has a wonderful way of talking about and to the land. (He's also an acclaimed author, most recently of *Heirlooms: Letters from a Peach Farmer*.) For Mas, the fruit he and his family grow is truly a labor of love. He knows every tree on the farm, its habits, and its history, inside out. The names themselves are wonderful: the Sun Crest, June Crest, and Gold Dust peaches, and the nectarines—the Rose Diamond and the Early Elegant Lady, among them. As we sat at the breakfast table on the porch of their farmhouse, shaded from the intense, bright heat of the day, we talked about how our friendship had grown out of those trees. Years ago, through a mutual friend, Bill Fujimoto, I first met Mas's peaches, and they led me to Mas.

Mas has always had his own ideas as an orchardist. In some ways, he's more a shepherd than a cultivator. His staff is his loyalty. While conventional growers pull out 15-year-old trees and move on to whatever seems to be the most popular new variety, Mas has set about ascertaining the true and natural life span of an organic, well-tended fruit tree. He follows the tree's instincts, a rather uncommon trait in a contemporary fruit grower. More than 300 Sun Crest peach trees on his farm are still producing delicious fruit at the grand old age of 40. (Bill Fujimoto hosted the landmark birthday party, at his Monterey Market in Berkeley.) "I even believe that when the trees were around 21 years old, I could detect a richer flavor in this peach," Mas told me. He pretty much single-handedly saved the Sun Crest from extinction. My worlds came together when Slow Food adopted the Sun Crest in its Ark of Taste project, which celebrates and reintroduces wonderful foods that are in danger of being lost forever in the food-industry shuffle.

Where others prize uniformity, Mas seeks out lesser-known heirloom varieties. (We talked about what "heirloom" really means in a world of easy marketing slogans, and his answer was so simple and sensible: "Something that's not trendy now.") Many heirlooms have been pushed out of production because they ripen "too early" or can't be coerced into producing big enough fruit, or because, like the Sun Crest, they have an extraordinary juiciness that makes them bruise easily. Mas is their rescuer and champion, luckily for us. Even before you taste it, you can recognize one of his peaches because it hasn't been "improved"; it has a natural variegated color, a pointy little tip, a suture (the indented crease that runs from the stem to the tip), and fuzz!

Mas and Marcy and their children, Nikiko and Korio, host a meal on their porch, surrounded by grapevines and stone fruit orchards.

Mas is a wholesaler and doesn't operate a CSA, but several years ago the family came up with the idea of an "adoption" program, in which people can come to the farm and pick Elberta peaches. "To me, it's the ultimate CSA," he said. "People apply to adopt a tree for a year, and the four of us sit down and review all the applications." How are the applicants judged? "They have to prove that they are in love with our peaches!" said Nikiko, who is going to carry on the family business. They also have to show that they've thought the thing through—they're going to end up with 500 pounds of fruit.

"The whole idea is that it's not a monetary exchange," Mas said. "It's relationship farming." Field notes are sent to the adopters throughout the year, so that they have a sense of the rhythms of this particular growing cycle; they learn why the fruit is blushing or perhaps why it has a more golden hue than in some other years. Then they come to the farm two Saturdays in a row and harvest their tree. Families come together, sometimes four generations, and Marcy cooks for everyone, and they share a meal in the orchard.

All my success as a restaurateur I owe to decades-long collaborations with people like Mas, who live what they grow. Though they have been forgotten by the food behemoths engaged in something called—how perfectly oxymoronic—factory farming, these dedicated practitioners are by no means gone. They are committed to natural, ripe, delicious, wholesome food and the relationships it fosters, season upon season. At a time when it has become irrefutably clear that human health and well-being cannot be considered apart from the health of the planet, they have a true understanding of what *sustainability* means to our future.

In these pages, you'll meet just a few of the many farmers who are the keepers of this faith. The work they do and the way they think about it are inspiring. They bring us back to our senses—and to the table.

Alice Waters

Mas visits a Gold Dust peach tree.

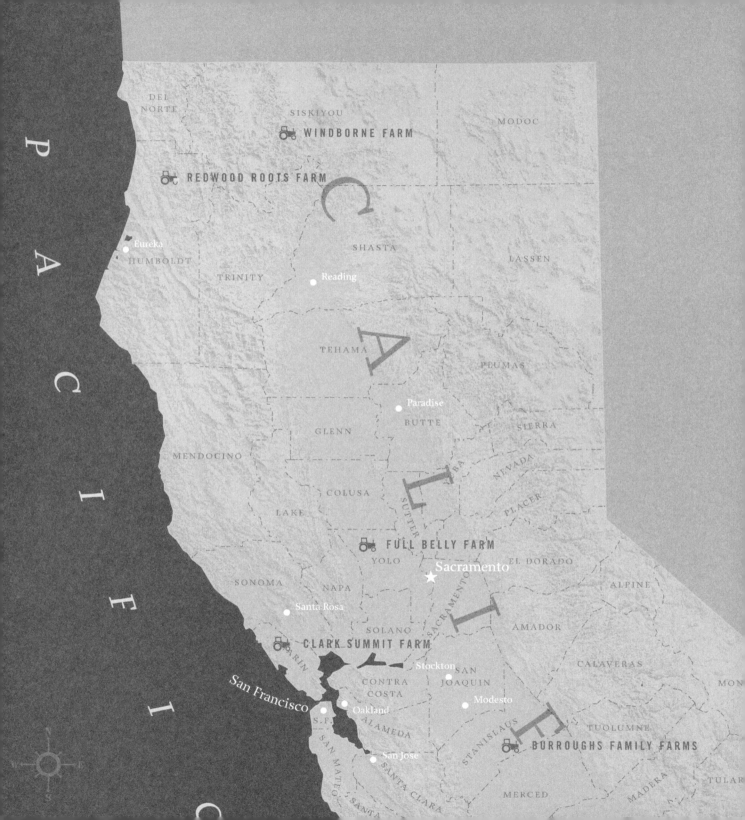

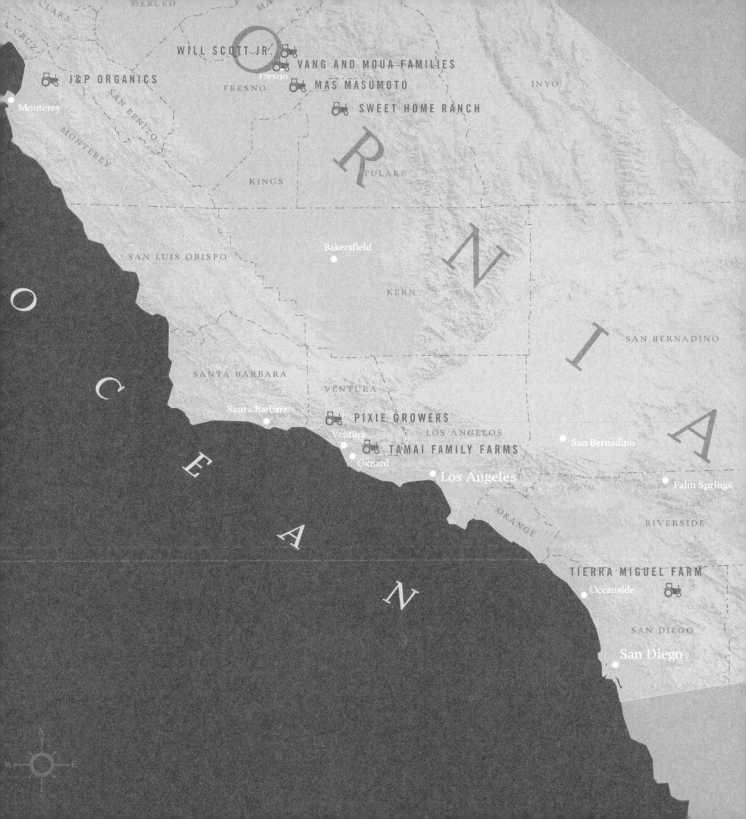

Farm Stories

Full Belly Farm
AN EARLY BLOOMER

YOLO COUNTY

In the upsurge of concern for all things sustainable, the small-scale organic farm has loomed large as an icon of embattled hope. Embattled, because many Americans have until quite recently been resigned to the belief that mega-scale, industrial agriculture—and its fatal chemical dependence—is pretty much here to stay. Now, word is spreading about thriving alternatives, and one need go no farther for a blast of rational exuberance than Full Belly Farm, 90 miles or so northwest of San Francisco, in the agricultural heartland of the Capay Valley. About 2 miles past the tiny crossroads of Guinda, a small sign points down a dirt track toward the farm's 250 acres of vegetables, fruits, nuts, grains, herbs, and flowers. Chickens, goats, pigs, sheep, and a few cows live here, too, along with the four partners who operate the farm,

their families, and an indeterminate number of friendly, noisy, mud-spattered dogs.

Paul Muller, who grew up on a family dairy farm in San Jose, and his wife, Dru Rivers, turned the first spade of earth at Fully Belly back in 1984. They began on 12 rented acres. Joined by fellow UC Davis alum Judith Redmond in 1989, they bought a parcel that they've gradually enlarged to its present size. The fourth partner, Andrew Brait, arrived as a farm intern in the early 1990s and found he couldn't leave; he and his wife, Anna, have been here ever since. Six children have grown up on the farm. Fifty full-time employees arrive for work each morning from their homes nearby. Paul Muller captures the tenor of the clan when he says, "We are personally in love with our farm. It is such a right livelihood for us."

Full Belly Farm is a living expression of both old and new: a traditional rural way of life

---

Judith Redmond, one of the Full Belly partners, picking artichokes for supper.

3

coupled with the practice of evolving ecosystem science. "An organic farm is not simply a place without chemical pesticides and fertilizers," says Judith, who's a natural scientist by training and has focused special attention on building indigenous-plant hedgerows for native pollinators. "We've worked to create a really good fertility and pest management program—so in some ways this farm looks like a pre–World War II farm, but in other ways it's really something entirely different." Paul brought his inherited talents to the enterprise but was determined to leave behind the previous generation's adoption of agricultural chemicals; he intended to farm as an environmental steward.

The question, at least in many other people's minds, was whether the ecological model could also foster a sustainable business. "It felt very risky," says Judith, who at the time they joined forces was executive director of a regional advocacy group, the Coalition with Family Farmers. "The organic movement was just beginning. I was working with people from UC Davis, from the farm bureau, from commodity boards and a lot of other agricultural institutions. On every panel, in every conversation, I heard the same thing: Anyone who thought they could make a living farming organically was very foolish."

Full Belly's farmers have not forgotten the hardships of the early years. "We couldn't imagine how we were even going to pay for the land," Judith says. The work was (and remains)

hard and unremitting. The partners' meetings were full of worry. The challenges of keeping the business safe and growing, making money, negotiating the weather and the regulatory demands—"it always felt like we were on the brink of disaster."

hat held the farmers together was their shared vision and an awareness that even as they were giving everything to the land, it was giving something extraordinary back—to them, in the pleasures of commitment and a nascent livelihood, and to the growing number of customers whose gratitude, interest, and support came in myriad forms, from the burgeoning Full Belly Community Supported Agriculture (CSA) membership to weekly conversations over the market stalls about the sweetness of a Full Belly peach or a newly discovered recipe for a favorite vegetable. "What we've been able to create—and what many farms can create—is a really wonderful quality of life for ourselves and our customers," says Judith, who oversees the market operations. "The current industrial paradigm is failing, and people everywhere are beginning to understand that this system is an alternative, a real alternative. It gives me the sense that we're doing something right."

A hedgerow in the foreground borders a flower field, with grapes and the stone fruit orchard in the distance.

KITCHEN
SCRAPS
HERE

Full Belly grows about 80 different crops in rotation year-round and picks them the day before they change hands. The farm's CSA now has 1,000 members, and Judith oversees additional weekly deliveries to 40 restaurants and stores and 20 wholesalers. Six thousand people descend on the farm every October for its famed Hoes Down Festival, now in its 21st year. "Are we insane or what?" says Judith. "We've talked about not doing it anymore, but we somehow keep doing it."

The challenges aren't any fewer these days—it's more that the setbacks have become part of the natural life and business cycle. "We've had disasters," says Judith. "We've had crop failures." Paul's account of a late freeze, in the farm's newsletter, had the quality of a letter to a family member away from home: "At 3 am, Andrew and I were moving plants inside of the greenhouse and starting water wherever we could. A few hours and a few degrees can change the realities for a season. In that short span of time, we appeared to have lost all of our 2008 stone fruit crop. The small fruit froze to their very heart and destroyed the developing seed therein. We have spent this last week checking fruit, and I can't seem to find any undamaged fruit. In addition all of the shoots on the grapes were burned black and the vines will need to start over— we might expect a small crop of grapes if the vines can recover and set some fruit. Figs, potatoes, and walnuts were also burned. It will take some time to evaluate the extent of the damage. Sorry."

The diversity of the farm's crops and the deep skills of its farmers have combined, especially in recent years, to create "the sense that there's a true stability here," Judith says. Somewhere along the way, the partners also discovered that their definition of *farmer* changed. "The obvious function of what we do is to grow food and fiber," she says. "But the more you think about the things that farms can do, the more you come to see that they can grow habitat, communities, new farmers, new environmental citizens. By this point, our internship program has had a pretty good rate of success. We now know former interns who are farmers in New York, Minnesota, Oklahoma, Alaska—and of course California. Some of them are kids who grew up in urban areas and have a sort of romantic idea about farming, and a lot of them last, I'm happy to say. But we also have young people who grew up on farms in the Central Valley. They want to go back and farm, but they know that the model their parents followed isn't right for them. And so they come here to learn about our model, to take it home to Madera, Merced, Fresno. We think that's pretty exciting."—Katrina Heron

Animal and vegetable, harvest and compost, and always, fresh eggs.

PREVIOUS PAGE: Judith and her husband, Thomas, host a meal on the terrace of their home on the farm.

How-To: Store It

Saving from Scratch

THERE ARE LOTS OF REASONS FOR cooking from scratch—the mastery of techniques, the pleasures of great taste, and, not the least, cost. § It seems obvious, but people forget: You can save a lot of money if you buy food you can store and use over time. For example, beans. Dried beans are far cheaper than the canned ones. To prepare them, get the biggest pot you have and put in a pound of beans (about 2 cups). Add 6 cups of cold water and let the pot sit on the countertop all day. When you get home, pour off the water the beans have been soaking in, then pour on 6 cups of fresh water, add ½ teaspoon of salt, and put the pot on the stove to boil. Let it boil for an hour and a half or so. After you've boiled the beans, you can just drop them in a container for storage in the fridge—not that much harder than opening a can and about a quarter of the price. § When tomatoes are in season, use them fresh instead of canned. Take a large, fully ripe tomato and grate it against a box grater (see recipe, page 149). The skin will peel off in your hand as you grate it. Use the fresh pulp in sauce, soups, and more. The sauce will be less acidic, fresher, and more watery than regular canned tomatoes. For a thicker sauce, boil until the liquid is reduced and has the desired consistency. § Buy more tomatoes than you could possibly eat fresh and save them—there are a couple of easy ways to do this that don't involve canning. You can freeze the tomatoes, either whole or cut into pieces. If you have a food dehydrator (see page 91), you can dry fresh tomatoes for use in soups and stews all year. Take masses of herbs, too, such as rosemary, oregano, and thyme, dry them by hanging or in the dehydrator, mix with salt in a food processor, and use for meat rubs and seasoning throughout the year.

Sweet Home Ranch
THE ORCHARD AS ART FORM

Under the gnarled plum trees in his oldest orchard, planted by his father, Paul Buxman stoops down and brings up a handful of the dark, damp soil.

"Here, smell this," he says, sighing happily, as if it were a plate of his biscuits, hot from the oven.

The dirt smells rich, deep. And clean. You almost want to take a bite.

"You can tell when a farm is biologically active, healthy," says Paul, pointing out all the other signs of a vibrant and balanced ecology on his 55 acres of apricot, nectarine, peach, plum, and grapefruit trees: ants busily mining the dirt and scavenging for the eggs of fruit-hungry aphids; earthworms tunneling and fertilizing; weeds alive with bees, ladybugs, and other beneficial insects; clover quietly fixing soil-enriching nitrogen; pest-eating birds nesting deep inside a trunk.

Sweet Home Ranch is nestled in California's agricultural heartland, near Fresno. It hasn't seen chemical pesticides or fertilizers for a quarter century. While farmers stretch back for generations on both sides of the Buxman family and they grew up on neighboring farms, neither Ruth nor Paul Buxman ever thought they'd be farmers themselves. Paul's first love was painting, and he went away to college to study art. "My teacher said, 'Don't try to make a living at it. Get a job and paint your life,'" advice that Paul took to heart. Working as a teacher and school principal, though, left him no time to paint. And then a timely call came from back home: His father needed help on the farm.

Paul Buxman believes the fruit should speak for itself.

13

"I said, 'Dad, I'm going to farm so I can paint,'" Paul recalls. And he does. His vivid impressionistic oil paintings of farm scenes hang by the score all over the Buxmans' modern-day log home, giving it the feel of an art gallery.

For her part, Ruth had left home and headed off to become a nurse and a Mennonite minister, caring for cancer patients and preaching in San Francisco and later Oregon. She didn't come back to the farm until much later, in 1994, as Paul's second wife.

By then, organic ruled at Sweet Home Ranch. In 1982, 2-year-old Wyeth had been diagnosed with leukemia, one of several such cases in Fresno, where the pesticide DBCP had been found in the groundwater. While no connection was ever confirmed, "it just made us think," Paul says. He did away with all the farm's chemicals and set out to relearn the art and science of farming.

"We started from scratch—there was no organic book," he says. "Look how far it's come! It's a revolution." Organic practices were considered so novel in the early 1980s that the Associated Press and *National Geographic* came out to see what the Buxmans were doing. As more farmers caught the wave, Paul founded California Clean, a certification program for family farms smaller than 100 acres. He counseled that healthy practices went beyond

merely avoiding chemical pesticides and fertilizers to encompass the whole farm environment—soil, earthworms, insects, birds, weeds. The practiced eye, Paul says, can spot an ecology that's in balance—or not—in a matter of minutes.

At its peak, California Clean had more than 100 members and enough of a reputation to command special labeling in stores. But then the focus and meaning of *organic* began to change, and the Buxmans' conscience dictated that Sweet Home Ranch would become an outlier once again.

It was the prospect of federal organic standards that prompted them, like many other small sustainable farmers, to weigh the pros and cons of an official seal of approval. For the Buxmans, organic was more than a list of regulated dos and don'ts; for one thing, says Paul, such limits beg to be pushed. But on a deeper level, organic was about trust, and relationships in the community, and doing the right thing, and, ultimately, respecting the soil—in other words, things that couldn't be codified.

Wyeth Buxman in the orchard. PREVIOUS PAGE: Pauline, Paul's mother, remembers when she and her husband, Albert, planted the first fruit trees. Jars of the Buxmans' preserves are hand-signed with pride.

Maybe the final straw was the notion that organic farmers could earn a premium for their fruit. It struck the Buxmans as just plain wrong. "We should never charge more for not poisoning people," Paul says.

And so, while large and newly christened organic farms boomed, the Buxmans went their own way: They gave up organic certification and tried to sell their fruit for a good price based on its flavor and quality and their sustainable practices.

The response was swift. "We lost our markets," Paul says. One steady customer, an East Coast natural food chain that was later bought by Whole Foods, told him, "If you're not [certified] organic, you're nothing to us."

He was undeterred. He sells his fruit, based on its taste and quality and methods of production, directly to independent markets and small chains nearby and in the San Francisco area, where he can forge relationships with buyers one by one. If the decision hurt financially, the Buxmans live more comfortably in their own skin, and Sweet Home Ranch continues to hum along according to the family's principles. Among these are to provide all the farm's workers with fresh meat and produce every

Rose Diamond nectarines, planted decades ago by Albert Buxman, are still producing beautiful fruit.

payday, to help them stretch their earnings; to hire the workers' kids to do the odd jobs around the farm that Wyeth and his friends once did as youngsters; and to invite at-risk teenagers to come out and get involved during the summers.

The Buxmans' philosophy of farming has the same through line as ever: nurture the land and be nurtured by it. Their belief was affirmed when Ruth's mother went to a nursing home to recuperate from heart surgery and simply stopped eating. The Buxmans brought her home to the farm and got her to eat fruit fresh off the trees. She bounced back and years later is going still strong. Now, Paul's mother, Pauline, has come to live with them. A typical morning finds the family gathered around the dining table, the lazy Susan revolving with bowls of gorgeous fresh-cut fruit. Paul bakes biscuits and pops the lids off jars of preserves. "I'm spoiled rotten," says Pauline, beaming.

The brightly hued preserves are Sweet Home Ranch's own—peach, plum, apricot, and nectarine, along with marmalade. A crop-damaging hailstorm inspired the new direction; now the tiny jars contribute about one-third of the farm's income. Each jar is hand signed by Paul, Ruth, or Wyeth, under a sketch of Ruth and the words "Fruit of the Spirit."—Carol Ness

How-To: Preserves

Jam Session

PRESERVES ARE EASY, says Paul Buxman: just fruit, sugar, and heat. You can find preserving instructions in many cookbooks or online. But the recipes themselves are often crude guides to the goal because the quality and sweetness of the fruit change with each batch. Here are tips from the Buxmans' kitchen for making your own.

★ Use only the best fruit—a good way to tell (other than eating it!) is to look for lots of sun freckling on the skin. Ask the grower to help you select a variety with high acid content, which boosts flavor.

★ Don't peel the fruit, except for peaches.

★ Cut the fruit into ¾-inch chunks and pour off the juice to shorten cooking time. (Juice can be boiled down into syrups.)

★ Cook in small batches—10 pounds or less. The jam cooks faster, and its color and flavor stay bright.

★ Add sugar after the fruit has broken down as it cooks. Pour off extra liquid to keep the preserves thick.

★ Don't use too much sugar. As a rule of thumb, use only half of what most recipes call for. Start with ½ cup per pound of fruit and add small amounts until the acid-sugar balance is pleasing. (Use cane sugar instead of beet sugar for better flavor.)

★ Stir fairly often using a wooden spoon.

★ Don't overcook. Preserves are almost done when bubbles surface and roll toward the center. Reduce the heat, pull out the spoon, and twirl twice above the pot; if jam drips off in more than one place, it's done. Overcooking will turn the jam brownish.

★ If you have room in the freezer, prepare ripe fruit in season and freeze it in batches; thaw and cook for fresh jam throughout the year.

Tamai Family Farms
GROWING UP TO BE FARMERS

"Wow, you're kind of young to be doing that, aren't you?"

That's the reaction Jason Tamai usually gets when he tells people he's a farmer. "When people say, 'What do you do?' my answer is always the big surprise." He's smiling broadly. "Then they usually say something like, 'So, uh, what do you wear to work? You have special clothes for that?'"

Jason, in his late 20s, is wearing his typical work uniform—a T-shirt, jeans, and a baseball cap. "It's hard to explain why I do what I do to people my age," he goes on. "I guess there's a notion that people don't grow up to be farmers anymore."

Aaron, Jason, and Julia Tamai at the farm.

For Jason, farming is a birthright; his mother, Gloria, talks about bringing him out to the strawberry fields when he was still too young to walk. She would sit him in a little chair under a makeshift sunshade while she weeded the rows. "It's in his blood," she says with pure satisfaction. "My next two kids were the same. My youngest is the only one who's not interested, and I know it's because we had more help by then and she didn't spend so much time out here with us."

These days, "out here" is two parallel strips—10 acres farmed conventionally and 5 organically—in the agricultural stronghold of Oxnard, about an hour's drive northwest of Los Angeles. In this southernmost corner of the vast Central Valley, the fields extend as far as the eye can see, and farm trucks and machinery still rule the road. But development has steadily encroached on arable land, and the Tamais, who are leasehold farmers, have had

23

to do some fancy footwork over the years to keep their tradition of family farming alive. Where once they were part of a large and convivial community, trading news and products, buying their milk from the dairy farm just down the road, and watching the kids grow up together, they can think of only a couple of other families who are still working the land as they do. The 15 acres the Tamais farm in Oxnard, growing a wide range of greens and root vegetables as well as corn and strawberries (including the prized Gaviotas), are hemmed in now by large operations cultivating monocrops such as celery, berries, and sod. The dairy farm is long gone. Orchards and flower fields, gone, too. A Highway 1 expansion and a new overpass wiped out a swath of their acreage and with it the roadside stand where Gloria first established her retail strawberry business.

Since then, Tamai Farms has branched out geographically, with two more parcels in Ventura—10 acres conventional and 8 organic—and more recently a plot of less than an acre in the Coachella Valley, where the higher temperatures are suited to growing tomatoes and peppers. (The Tamais are especially proud of their Tough Boy tomato, a Japanese variety with unusual sweetness and low acidity.)

Jason's father, Steve, has farmed all his life, as did his father and grandfather. While still a teenager, Jason's grandfather was sent to the Manzanar Internment Camp. One gets the sense that this part of the family history is private, referred to only in passing as the era of "the concentration camp" before the conversation turns back with ease to tales of more mundane hardships and perseverance. After the war, the Driscoll strawberry company was looking for growers, and Steve's father and brother signed on. The father hoped his sons would grow a farming business together. He got half his wish: Steve became a farmer, while his brother became a doctor. Jason points out that his grandfather's dream has only skipped a generation: He and his brother, Aaron, will take over Tamai Farms, and their sister Julia may well stay on to run it with them.

They'll inherit a name that emblematizes high quality and an unsurpassed work ethic. Their mother, who christened the retail business Gloria's Fruits and Vegetables, is known at the Los Angeles farmers' markets and in the kitchens of many area restaurants as a purveyor of all things fresh and delicious. A typical story involves the recent fight that broke out at the market over her cherry tomatoes because there weren't enough to go around. Her solution was

Gloria and Steve Tamai met as teenagers and built the business together.

to ration them. "I told everyone they were going to have to share," she says in a firm, motherly tone.

Reflecting on the fact that his grandfather opted not to buy land when it was affordable and that his father wanted to buy when it wasn't, Jason believes the future of Tamai Farms depends on land ownership. Other costs—fuel for transport, of course, but also the rising price of organic fertilizers—concern him as well. His generation has the technical knowledge and experience they need, he says, but the marketplace is more challenging than ever. Anticipating demand is key, and demand is more unpredictable for the small producer. "I think it's harder now to be a bad farmer but also harder to be a good businessperson," he says. This fourth generation's plan is to home in on niche staples that command a fairly consistent price and audience, such as their mother's famous cherry tomatoes. Restaurants already seek out Tamai products, often calling ahead to order. The family has set aside a small plot of land for experimenting with crops requested by their most supportive chefs. "That's how I discovered Swiss chard," says Jason.

Both Jason and sister Julia tried the desk-job route. Neither lasted long—they describe being tied to a computer and phone in the office environment as a form of interminable and alien purgatory. "At some point I just thought, 'I can't do this anymore,'" Jason recalls. "You find yourself wondering what it's like outside. I like being out here. The hours suck, but you kind of get bit by it—it's what you want to do. There's a lot of freedom, you're your own boss, and you get to be with your family. It's a total team effort, 7 days a week except for November and December. You get into a rhythm, and it feels normal."

As Jason sees it, the business plan and the 7-day workweek will get the Tamais only so far. He and his siblings have to do something more: Persuade their own age group to eat real food. "My generation is used to seeing things that are big and smooth and all look the same. The Italian green Romano bean scares people. It's long and wide and flat; it's unfamiliar. And it's the best bean there is.

"I'm trying to show people my age how much better an heirloom tomato tastes. They say, 'It's got wrinkles!' And I say, 'Yeah, it does—you should try it.'"—Katrina Heron

---

The Tamais grow an array of greens, including kale, and are known for their Gaviota strawberries.

Burroughs Family Farms
THE COWS COME HOME

The Burroughs family story is a romance—a persistent, generations-long love affair with agriculture. If agriculture seems antiseptic or unlovable, consider what it means for the Burroughses: green grass, cattle, milk, almonds, eggs, children, horses, 4-year-olds who can ride better than they can run, and, most of all, a family that lives and works together.

Situated between the farms that Rosie and Ward run with their children is another operation—the dairy that they originally came to this eastern edge of the valley to support. Ward's brother, Bruce Burroughs, runs this farm, a large industrial dairy where hundreds of white and black cows crowd together on

Jed, son of Christina and Brian Bylsma and grandson of Rosie and Ward Burroughs.

feedlots of bare earth and manure. Machines pump milk from udders all day and, under lights, through the night as well. The Burroughs farms on either side couldn't look more different. Brown and black cows make lazy circuits around green paddocks, heads down, vacuuming up grass. Organic almond orchards cover the rolling hills above them.

When Ward and Rosie moved to this farm to grow feed for the cows in the high-production dairy, they had no idea they would end up farming at the other end of the spectrum. "If you'd told me then that I'd be making organic milk and almonds, I'd have laughed in your face," Ward says. There was no single moment of epiphany; instead, a number of small things built up to their eventual conversion. There was a seed for Rosie in her heritage—her family is part Ute, the Native American tribe of southern Utah and Colorado and northern New Mexico; and part Basque, the European people who

29

became famous in the American West for their skill as shepherds. Both groups depended on the environment for their livelihood, and as a result, Rosie learned early on that stewardship of the land was a fundamental virtue. As for Ward, he'd always been something of a cowboy. He loved throwing a lasso from horseback and moving a herd of cattle. Dairies that kept cows in confinement didn't hold much joy for him. Among farmers, the people who run cattle have a reputation for maintaining a stubborn independence at all costs. While the pig and chicken farms are dominated by a few major corporations, no business has been able to organize, intimidate, or bribe the cowboys. For Ward, that meant he kept a herd of beef cattle long after it ceased to be profitable.

When their oldest child, Christina, was finishing college, Rosie told Ward that if they didn't bring her into the family business, they would lose her. So Ward suggested that Christina investigate whether there was any way to make cows on pasture profitable. As part of her due diligence, she went to New Zealand, where many dairies keep their cows on grass. Two years later, the Burroughses began building Full Circle Dairy—a farm that would bring dairying back to the way Christina's great-grandfather had farmed.

The news spread rapidly—in the Central Valley a farmer who tries to compete by letting the cows graze seems just about as crazy as a farmer in Iowa who plows down his corn to build a baseball field. "Everyone was watching me," Christina says. "Nobody knew if it would work, and, you know, I was a girl." Word spread far enough to reach the ears of the recruiters at Organic Valley—a cooperative that sells milk from organic family farms. But when the people from Organic Valley asked the Burroughses if they would consider going organic, they said no. "More than anything, I wasn't prepared for it mentally," Ward says. "Just going to grass was already way out in left field. Organic was even farther out there." Instead, the Burroughses sold to a cheese plant, receiving the same price for their milk as any of the industrial dairies that dot the Central Valley. Amazingly, it worked. While Full Circle Dairy couldn't bring in the revenue of the industrial dairies, it also didn't have an industrial dairy's overhead: The Burroughses didn't have to pay constant veterinary bills for sick cows and found that their animals lived two to three times longer than the heavily milked Holsteins. "When times were good, we could make a little money," says Ward. "And when times were bad—well then everybody is losing money on every gallon they sell. And in that situation, it's better if you aren't selling thousands of gallons."

A family-brand bottle from the days when the Burroughs dairy distributed its own milk. PREVIOUS PAGE: *A few of the grass-pastured herd.*

After that, organic didn't seem so far out there anymore. Ward had been worried that too many cows would die without antibiotic treatment. But after he saw how much healthier the cows on pasture were, this fear evaporated. When another 300 acres opened up, Rosie insisted that they should turn this land into another dairy—and make this one organic. It was the youngest child, Zeb, and his wife, Meredith, who took charge of this farm. In the meantime, middle child Benina took over the almond orchards and began converting them to organic trees—and Christina married Brian Bylsma and convinced him to join her at Full Circle as the family converted that dairy, too.

The family are still very much figuring things out as they go. Christina and Brian are working with portable chicken coops (they can be moved to follow grazing cows so that the chickens can grow fat on flies and their larvae); Benina is experimenting with irrigation, compost, and beneficial insects, encouraging the latter by allowing some groundcover to grow beneath the trees in the orchards; and they all are working to perfect the art of managing the pastures. The Burroughses readily admit that they've never stopped making mistakes, but it's clear that they are up for whatever challenges lie ahead.

As they linger over the remains of one family dinner, a beautiful tableau unfolds: The treble screams of the half-dozen children come cutting through the night, seconds before they appear in the flesh, triumphantly presenting fist-size frogs for inspection.—Nathanael Johnson

Rosie and Ward at a summer meal. His grandfather launched the family dairy business in 1906. PREVIOUS PAGE: If you're a Burroughs, you can rope and ride. The portable chicken coops follow the grazing cows.

Issue: Pasteurization

The Raw and the Cooked

SPEND TIME WITH THE BURROUGHS FAMILY and you'll see lots of people drinking raw milk, from toddlers sucking on sippy cups to grandparents downing glass after glass. Raw milk comes straight from the cows, which means that unlike most milk you find in supermarkets, it has not been pasteurized. To pasteurize fresh raw milk, producers heat it up, which kills off the natural microbes that are plentiful in raw milk. (Microbes become part of the picture as soon as the hot milk leaves the cow—from the animal's udders, the air, and any surface the milk touches.) In most states, it is illegal to sell raw milk—California is one of the few exceptions. § The pasteurization laws are there for good reason. At the turn of the century, pasteurization laws were enacted around the country, as tuberculosis infections often developed in humans who drank milk from animals that were in the late stages of the disease. Since then, animal husbandry techniques have improved significantly, but the pasteurization laws remain in effect, and they do protect people from a number of harmful bacteria that can get in milk in dairies that may not have tip-top hygiene practices. Raw-milk advocates argue that pasteurization isn't necessary if cows eat grass rather than high-energy feeds and graze in pastures rather than lying in their own manure in a feedlot. And, proponents say, raw milk is more likely to make you healthier than to give you a disease. There is some emerging science that suggests that raw milk may protect people—especially children—from autoimmune disorders such as asthma, eczema, and allergies. Unfortunately, it's children and the elderly who become sickest if something goes wrong. Tuberculosis is much less common, but *E. coli* and salmonella can pose a serious threat. § If milk is contaminated through contact with these microflora, the risk to healthy adults of becoming seriously sick is almost nil. Interestingly, in a couple of the cases in which public health officials tracked disease outbreaks back to raw milk, they found that people who had been drinking the milk for a long time had an immunity to the sickness. Being exposed to low levels of bacteria may have primed their immune systems. § In the state of California, the raw-milk issue is a touchy subject for consumers and legislators—Democrats are trying to pass legislation that would allow small farmers to continue selling raw milk, while Republicans are favoring the calls from big dairy associations and food safety inspectors to end the practice. It's difficult to predict the outcome of this debate, because while everyone can agree that public safety is essential, not everyone can agree on how best to guarantee it. But it seems likely that even if farmers do indeed lose the right to sell their milk in supermarkets, they are likely to go on providing the genuine raw article to their friends and neighbors.

Will Scott Jr.
A SPIRIT OF PERSEVERANCE

FRESNO COUNTY

"I t takes time for people to gather around the idea and understand its importance," says Will Scott Jr. It's been about a decade since Will first started driving every weekend from his farm in Fresno up north to West Oakland, his truck laden to the brim with fresh organic produce. The trip takes him 3 hours each way. It is time he has never given away lightly: "A farmer should be able to do what he does best—work the land," he says. Yet the way he sees it, circumstances require him to be an emissary or, perhaps more accurately, a missionary. West Oakland is a low-income, mostly African American community with virtually no access to fresh food. And so, despite invitations to join other farmers' markets in the Bay Area, Will chooses to bring his wares to the one where he feels they are needed most.

On a hot Saturday in early summer, Will *is* the market—a lone umbrella staked out on the burning asphalt, marking the spot where he hopes there will one day be a thriving fresh-foods bazaar. Some Saturdays more farmers show up—as the summer wears on, the numbers tend to increase—but there's no telling how many will come or for how long, and when the umbrellas dwindle, so does the momentum. "Shoppers want to see a crowd of sellers, and farmers want to see a crowd of buyers," Will says, "so each is kind of waiting for the other to commit. The way I see it, you've got to stick."

One of his largest potential customer bases lives right across the street, in the Mandela Gateway Housing Development. He knows from experience that he can convert these residents; he will just have to do it one by one. "Someone

---

"When you talk about food," says Will, "you're talking about quality but also about availability. They have to go together."

41

will walk over here and say, 'I've been watching you out of my window. What are you doing here? What are you selling?' And then I'll show them"—fruit, tomatoes, onions, sweet corn, sweet potatoes, black-eyed peas, collards, mustard greens, okra, peppers. He smiles. "Once they come over here and talk to me, I have them. They see that my produce is fresh and good, and I don't use chemicals, and then they understand and they come back. But it takes time. It takes time for people to learn that this is the way to eat, not the fast-food way."

It is something Will was brought up knowing. His grandfather was a sharecropper in Oklahoma, and his father, who moved the family to Fresno, worked in a variety of jobs while farming on the side. "People talk about organic, but I call it natural," Will says. "My parents never used any chemicals—we composted, we used the nutrients the land provides when you take care of it." Growing up, he worked summers cutting grapes and chopping cotton. Farming was in his blood but not in his plans. After attending junior college, he enlisted in the navy and went to Vietnam with the submarine corps. On his return, he went back to school at Fresno State and became an engineer with what was then the Pacific Telephone Company. At the outset of a long career as a technical professional, he bought a piece of land—5 acres along a two-lane road heading north out of town—and farmed it in his spare time, though he notes with some

amusement, "there really is no such thing as part-time farming." Retiring from his desk job in the mid-'90s, he felt the pull of the land and decided to devote his full attention to it—"and as I tell my family, it's like going from the skillet into the fire."

His decision was equal parts entrepreneurial and political. He saw clearly the market for the sage producer of "specialty" items—offerings that the large growers often ignore. Will saw variety as a strategic advantage. His black-eyed peas, which have become famous in the region, are a case in point. "'Local' can be a big selling point, too. I sell with the season. And I can ask my buyers, 'What do you need? What do you want that I don't have?' Some of them even bring you seeds. I can make adjustments to meet the demand." Black-eyed pea sales shot up when he started offering them preshelled: "The older folks like to shell their own—it's kind of like therapy for them—but I learned that the younger ones want them ready to cook."

As the grandson of a sharecropper and a witness himself, during the 1980s and '90s, to the period that saw the greatest loss of black farmers in the century, Will had no illusions about the African American farmer's precarious status. In 1999, the USDA acknowledged

Will farms as his parents did: organic compost, no chemicals.

long-standing discrimination in agreeing to settle a class-action suit (known as the Pigford case) brought on behalf of African American farmers who had been routinely denied access to federal support, much of it in the form of Farmers Home Administration loans. Many had lost their farms in foreclosure or bankruptcy while waiting for help that never came, while federal assistance poured out to the agricultural sector overall. The decline in the number of American farms is staggering; attrition in the African American segment is disproportionately so. Today, about 18,000 African American farms remain nationwide, out of the roughly 2 million total.

But Will isn't focused so much on the past as he is on the future; he's thinking about a category of farmer known in the vernacular as "returning"—an experienced hand who either still owns or has access to land but gave up the trade for want of reward—and, especially, about the next generation. "This is a multi-billion-dollar business in California," he notes. "We need to entice young African Americans to get involved, and not just in farming but in all the other aspects of agriculture as well."

As founder and president of the African American Farmers of California (current Fresno-area membership: 33), Will has a new part-time job helping to ensure that his constituents have access to all available information and support from the USDA. The agency that was once widely viewed by black farmers as "the last plantation" is pledging assistance through newly funded initiatives such as a demonstration site that Will's group will operate on a parcel of local land. It will be a place for aspiring farmers to learn firsthand about sustainable practices and the business of farming—how to direct-sell whenever possible, whether to restaurants or at farmers' markets, and how to forge links with community hubs such as churches and schools. Will also envisions the creation of a local producers' cooperative that will assume a leadership role in marketing and distribution, as well as provide storage, processing facilities, and a retail store.

As for the West Oakland Farmers' Market, "it's a struggle," Will admits. "If I was doing it for the money, I wouldn't do it. But I'm not. I'm doing it because fresh food needs to be accessible to this community. I believe the potential is there. It's like farming itself—you have to take it step-by-step. A lot of the time, the shortcuts don't work out too well. Take care of it, though, and the plants will jump tall."
—Katrina Heron

The Scott brothers weed rows of peppers with hand hoes.

Issue: Certification

Organic Inc.

LAST YEAR SAFEWAY ROLLED OUT ITS LINE of organic foods, branded as Safeway O. Now, when shoppers walk down the aisles, they find organic products with brands and packages that look almost identical to the conventional ones. Gone are the days of funky do-it-yourself packages from renegade producers. If you compare an organic carton of milk with a conventional one, you'll find only one major difference: the price tag. It's no surprise that customers wonder if they're really getting anything different when they opt for the premium product. § Farmers are wondering the same thing. Some are eschewing organic certification because they feel the standards don't adequately differentiate their style of farming from industrial practices; a small farmer growing organic produce for the local market shouldn't be classified identically with a large organic producer from another country or even another hemisphere. Some chafe at the recent rules and bureaucracy imposed by an authority they feel is a Johnny-come-lately. And then there are those who feel that their relationship with their customers negates the need for any label. § The National Organic Program, which is run by the USDA and supplies certification for the USDA Organic seal, does make significant distinctions that affect farm habitat and, according to several studies, the healthfulness of the food. If a food bears this seal—or is labeled organic—it must have been certified to contain at least 95 percent organic ingredients. But what's the legal definition of *organic ingredients*? That's impossible to answer in full without making long lists of allowed and forbidden practices. The short version: foods grown without synthetic pesticides or fertilizers. But if you dig down into this list, you can find problems. The USDA law allows restricted use of Chilean nitrate, for example, because it's mined from a natural source, rather than chemically synthesized. But if farmers overuse Chilean nitrate, the environmental effects are about the same as those of chemical fertilizers. § As for animals, certification requires farmers to use organic feed and to treat animals humanely. (Industrial meat producers are issued the same humane treatment rules, but it's an empty gesture—compliance is voluntary.) Livestock raised organically must also have access to pasture or the outdoors. But some producers follow the letter of the law rather than the spirit, crowding the animals on feedlots and providing only a postage-stamp-size plot of grass for infrequent access. § If the label is absent, it's worth finding out whether the producer is operating with chemicals or just with hardheaded independence. (Some farmers have their own calculus for what's acceptable—they will use fungicides on their berries, for example, but won't use herbicides.) Anecdotal evidence suggests that since the upsurge of Big Organic, more small farmers are practicing some or even all of the requirements without the official stamp of approval. So at least for the time being, the best way to gauge the pureness of a product may be to get to know the producer and just ask.

Windborne Farm
GRAIN SPECIALIST

Jennifer Greene built her farm to answer the question "How many people can one woman feed?" The answer, for now, is about 100. Fueled by a tiny, diverse agricultural ecosystem, Jennifer grows more than 40 types of cereals and legumes that she plants, harvests, threshes, grinds, and then sells directly to home bakers and cooks. She works alone, save the occasional assistance of a neighbor or farm intern. She chose cereals, she says, because "grains are the easiest crops to grow, and also I always thought they were the most relaxed crops." Because grains take longer to grow, "they are just not as frenetic as vegetables." The long winter pauses also give her time to be with her three sons and a chance to regroup before the preparations for spring planting begin again. After nearly a decade of direct-marketing her grain, Jennifer has a flourishing CSA membership of bakers who buy her freshly milled flours as "grain shares."

"I've told people who want to join my CSA program that if they're not really into baking bread, they might as well not bother," she says. Indeed, joining the Windborne CSA is pledging to a vigorous and creative bread-baking discipline, as each delivery contains a mix of wheat, rye, and oat flour, along with lentils, chickpeas, and the occasional exotic grain, such as teff or amaranth. She also grows dry corn and pumpkins (for the seeds). Each year, Windborne Farm distributes 150 pounds of grain and legumes to each customer in 10 deliveries, all of it packaged in small brown lunch bags that Jennifer labels with a ball-point pen, seals with tape, and packs into grocery bags for the drive to the CSA's pickup points.

Jennifer at the picnic table, surrounded by bed rolls.

Jennifer's farming techniques were heavily influenced by the biodynamic practices she witnessed during a 2-year stint at Live Power Community Farm in Mendocino County and, before that, while working at Full Belly Farm in Yolo County (see page 3). She bought her farm 5 years ago, moving north from the Capay Valley, where she had started a grain-farming business on leased land. Windborne Farm is pretty much as far north as you can go and still farm in California—it's at the heart of one of the many valleys snaking off and around Mount Shasta. A 30-acre patchwork of variegated and often unusual crops, her plot is immediately identifiable amid thousands of acres of alfalfa, and her horse-drawn plow completes the contrasting picture. The Shasta farmers once grew only dry-farmed (unirrigated) wheat—there is still a remnant of the centuries-old mule trail they cut to cart their grain to market in Arcata, bringing back loads of sea salt and whiskey. But farmers here stopped growing grains 60 years ago, when the installation of irrigation systems made commodity-crop growing much more lucrative. Still, the region's farmers remember the days of grain farming, and they support Windborne as a sign of renaissance, lending Jennifer a helping hand and stopping by to share coffee and stories.

Jennifer knows a lot about a lot, practically speaking. Her philosophy is to teach simply by doing. While her neighbors continue to plant alfalfa year after year, plowing with giant tractors and pumping the soil with commercial fertilizers to keep it productive, she farms each section of Windborne in three rotations without chemical inputs, so that her winter grains are followed by spring legumes and then the field is left to rest for one season. The farm isn't certified organic or biodynamic; Jennifer doesn't have much interest (or place much trust) in external labeling systems. She operates from a fierce desire to farm and live according to her principles and strives for economic self-sufficiency on those same very personal terms; her operation grosses just over $40,000 a year, three-quarters of it from her grain shares and one-quarter from the fees she charges school groups to visit the farm. The family lives close to the economic edge, comfortably. While she's talking about how she changed her billing cycle for the Windborne CSA, her son Jason interjects exuberantly that "in February we ran out of money!" causing the two of them to burst into laughter. Jennifer sends an e-mail every year to her CSA members, detailing the

Jennifer's son Rafael. PREVIOUS PAGE: A farm intern at lunch. Sons Jason (rear) and Juan sit on swing chairs suspended from the trees.

family's expenditures and income, and explaining (for the benefit of the city dwellers on the list) why it's important to a farming family's bottom line to keep a few goats for milk and meat.

Last year, Jennifer trimmed expenses by growing her own vegetables and at the same time augmented her income by selling her own bread in the local market for the first time. Each element of her farming and processing operation can tell a story of economic ingenuity—the bins she uses to store grain, which she got free of charge from a corn syrup processing facility; the combine she spotted rusting in a neighbor's field and spent a winter restoring to health. In the past, she has also earned extra money by running a summer camp, taking a group of children from the city hiking in the Shasta foothills with a goat tagging along. It sounds like a surreal and wonderful experience—every morning and night the kids milked the goat, made fresh cheese over the campfire, and played "mountain baseball" in open glades in the forest while the goat napped in the center of the diamond. She also developed and ran a cake camp where she baked daily with a group of adolescent girls— she cracks a wide grin recalling the fun they had baking "fancy" cakes in her outdoor wood oven.

Family life is lived mostly outdoors as soon as the weather warms—with bedrolls laid out on the open grass for Jennifer's two youngest sons, Rafael and Jason, and a pup tent staked out on the farmhouse lawn for the intern. Meals, too, are eaten outdoors as often as the weather permits. The family's picnic table sits next to the hand-built bread oven, where a slow-burning fire cooks flat breads made from whole grain flour, and fresh asparagus and zucchini roast in cast-iron pans. Rafael and Jason roll the flat breads and slide them into the oven using a wooden peel, while the sound of the oldest son, Juan, playing the piano drifts out from the farmhouse. Jennifer sets out cold mason jars of chickpea puree to start the meal, which is slowly augmented as the pans of roasted vegetables emerge from the oven. Juan joins in as the asparagus arrives at the table, and after the vegetables are gone and scraps of bread have been used to sop up the oil and juices lingering in the pans, everyone finishes dinner with a salad. The farm interns and Jennifer's boys immediately reconvene after dishwashing for a game of soccer on the lawn, dodging two aged Nubian goats that kneel as they forage for grass on the playing field. Laughter and energy move from the dinner table out into the evening air, a testament to the world of plenty Jennifer has built—singlehandedly— on Windborne Farm.—Anya Fernald

Jason making flat breads. PREVIOUS PAGE: Jennifer feeding her Nubian goats.

Clark Summit Farm
GROWING GREENER PASTURES

MARIN COUNTY

Liz Cunninghame and her husband, Dan Bagley, live in the weathered white farmhouse where Liz grew up, on the same land where her father's cows grazed and her grandparents kept a small dairy. Her own four children grew up in a low brown house just down the hill from the family homestead.

Their 160 acres in the coastal hills of West Marin have been in the family since 1916. But when Liz inherited the farm in the 1990s, it was hard to imagine how a small dairy could keep that family legacy alive. With its abundant grasslands and windy, foggy summers, this stretch of land has traditionally been a place where agriculture meant grazing animals, mainly beef and dairy cattle. But in modern times, that kind of agriculture has become a stretch for small farmers and ranchers. Dairy farms sell primarily into the mass distribution market, where prices are unpredictable and profits low. Young beef cattle raised on the ranches of West Marin tend to go to feedlots in far-off places like Idaho for fattening, returning to Bay Area meat counters as neatly packaged rib eyes and hamburger.

Surely, Liz and Dan thought, there had to be a way to break that chain, a way to reconnect their farm with the dinner tables of the large and sustainably minded population living in the suburbs and cities just to the south. The organic farm movement had swept across the Bay Area, but these hills were too cold for fruits and vegetables. The same people who sought out fresh and seasonal produce, though, had begun seeking out meat, poultry, and eggs raised on local pastures.

Dinner is on for some of the 90 pigs born on the farm this year, outside the A-frame where they were farrowed.

59

Liz had always loved animals—and so an idea and a new farm were born. "We bought 10 chickens, just for us," says Liz. "We liked it!"

The next year, they bought 300 and started selling the eggs at farmers' markets and the general store in the tiny town of Tomales. People couldn't get enough of the eggs' deep orange yolks; their clean, rich flavor; and the fact that the hens that laid them weren't warehoused but lived regular, chickenlike lives.

Foods grown this way cost more, but customers recognized the benefits to the environment, as well as to the animals. Pasturing creates an endlessly sustainable cycle: The sun grows the grass, the animals eat it, and their waste fertilizes new grass. Adopted on a national scale, the practice would slash the use of synthetic fertilizers to grow feed and keep the runoff from poisoning waterways. And emptying feedlots would shut down the gigantic manure lagoons that pollute the air and water.

Liz and Dan took their land organic and started adding beef cattle, which roam the range; chickens for meat, in movable pens; and then pigs, which stampede happily down the hill when they think Dan might be bringing the day's whey from a nearby organic cheese maker. "It seemed like an old-new way to do things," says Liz. Soon Dan was a weekly fixture at weekend farmers' markets, selling grass-fed pork chops, steaks, chickens, and eggs.

They renamed the place Clark Summit Farm, after an old railway stop that used to be on the property for trains carrying cream to San Francisco. Customers dropping by the farm to pick up a suckling pig can see the family's dogs guarding the chicken pens from coyotes and hawks. Visitors keep a safe distance from Bosworth, the 400-pound boar (daddy to 90 piglets from 27 sows this year), who hangs out down near the pond/wallow. They may catch a glimpse of Biscuit, the pretty Jersey cow that keeps the family in milk and butter, feeding in the blackberry thicket down by the road.

Dinner around the old oval table means a 12-pound farm-raised ham, grilled to crusty crunchiness by Dan; fresh white cheese from Latte the Nubian goat; early tomatoes from nearby farms; and butter and vanilla ice cream courtesy of Biscuit. Everyone cleans his or her plate, and Dan sums it up: "Everything tastes good when it's farmed right."

For all this pastoral tranquillity, though, Liz and Dan have learned that raising animals the old-new way is backbreaking—and sometimes heartbreaking—work, 24/7. Water and feed

"I'm glad I found someone crazy enough to do this with me," says Liz of her husband, Dan. Bella (top right) guards the hens. American buff geese in the barnyard. Week-old chicks under heat lamps.

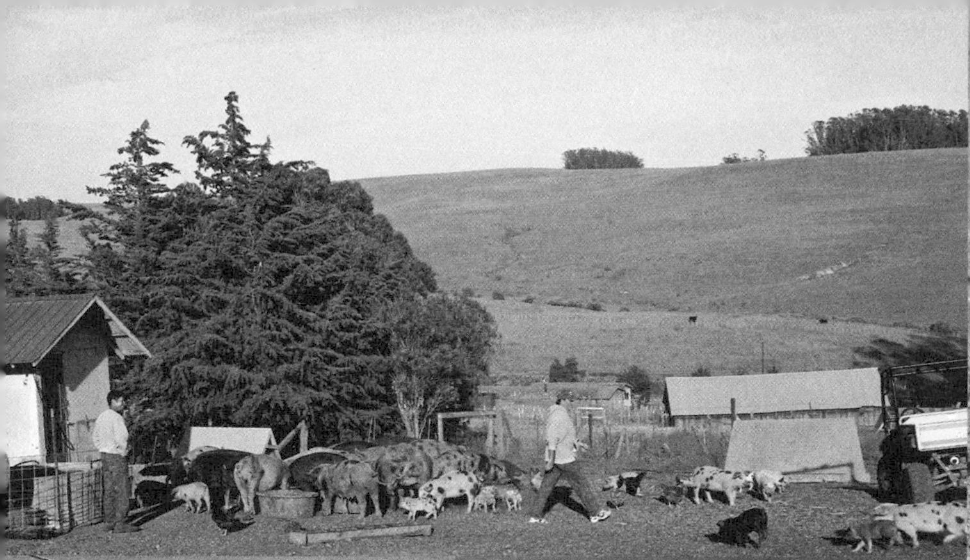

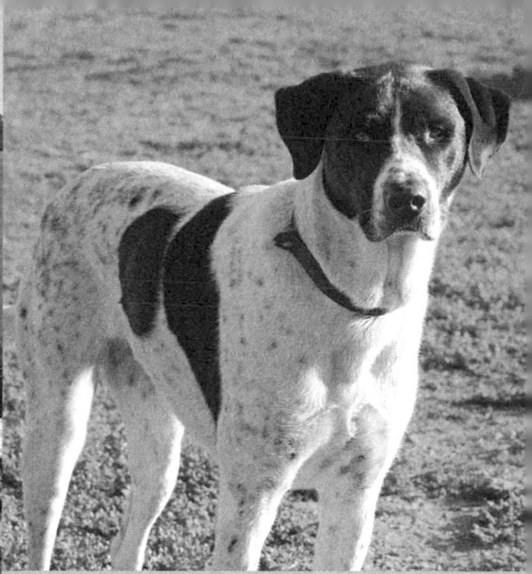

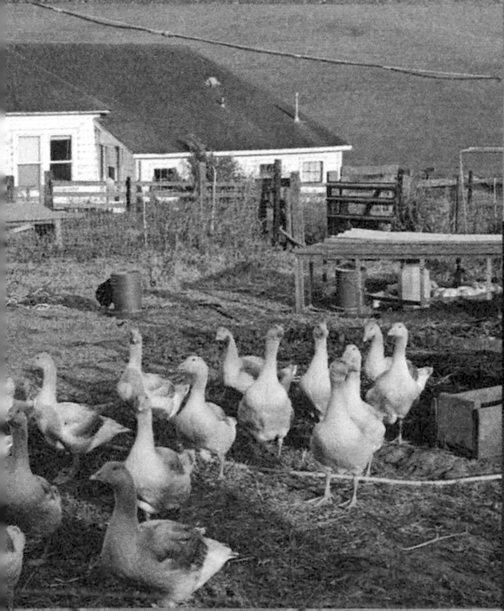

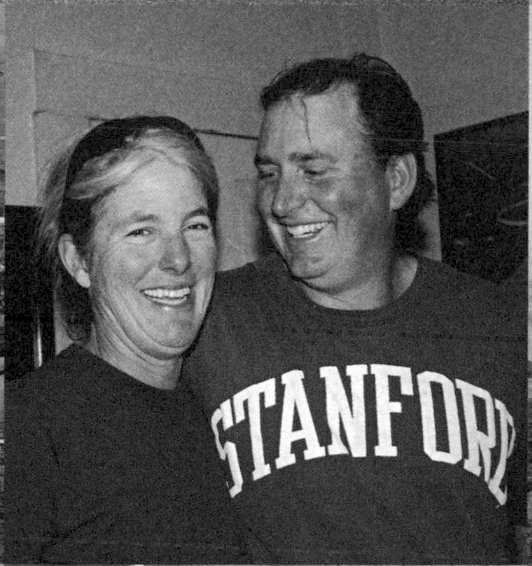
STANFORD

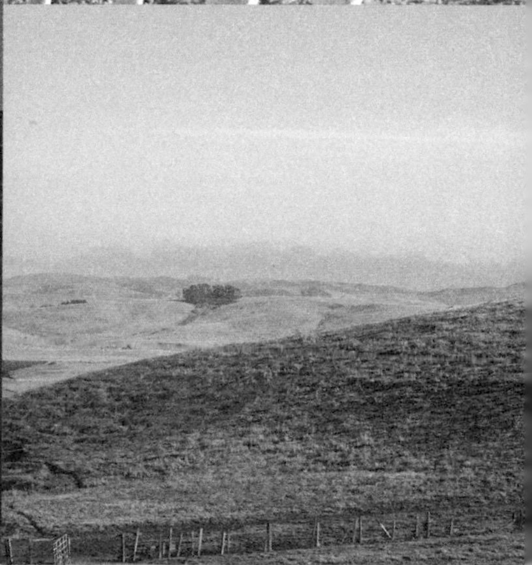

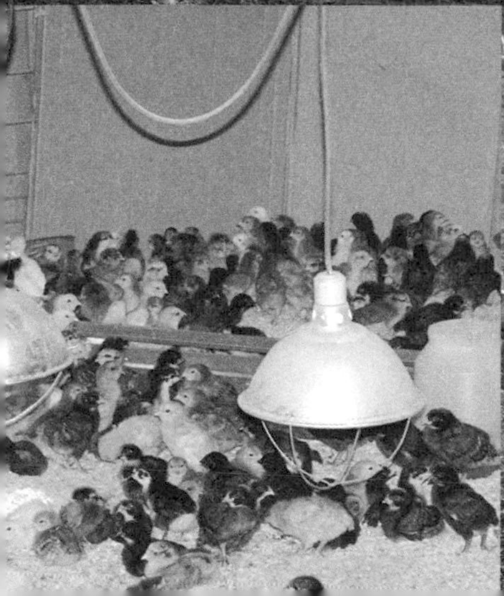

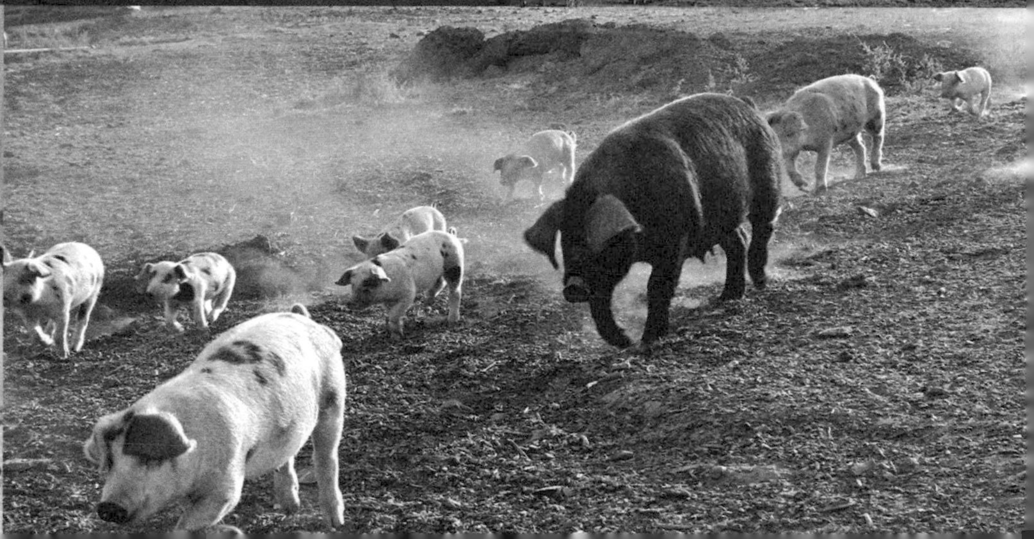

have to be hauled up the hill to the hens, cattle, and pigs. The chickens mow down their patch of pasture so fast that their pens and laying houses are always being moved. Biscuit wants milking. And eggs need collecting, every day.

Disaster can strike at any time—like the winter storm that took down half the hay barn, or the spring heat wave that took out the broiler chickens just as they were ready for market.

"People can leave paperwork on their desks at the end of the day," says Liz. "But I've got lives I've got to take care of." Still, the farm's growth has allowed her to quit her other job at a nearby organic dairy. Dan still works at the Tomales school, to keep a safety net (and health insurance) under them.

Farmers' markets are a good outlet for their products, but Dan can be at only one at a time. A few stores now carry the farm's eggs, so Liz drives a truckload to San Francisco every Wednesday, rushing home in time to milk the cow and gather more eggs. In early 2008, Clark Summit became one of the first local meat producers to adopt the CSA model, following the lead of the popular farm programs in which subscribers pick up a weekly box of fruits and vegetables. Clark Summit CSA members receive a monthly box of frozen beef, chicken, and pork, delivered to two pickup points in the city. This means a guaranteed, paid-up-front market for the producers and a steady supply for consumers who otherwise have a hard time finding these meats. But the logistics have proven daunting, such as dividing large animals fairly, for example. You don't want some customers get steak while others get stew. And federal regulations designed for the feedlot-packinghouse system add a layer of difficulty for small producers, a factor that's slowing the spread of farms like Clark Summit.

For Liz and Dan to sell steaks, chops, and other individual cuts of meat, animals have to be slaughtered in a USDA-inspected facility. But the consolidation of the meat industry has shuttered most of the small slaughterhouses that once were common in farm towns. Most of those that remain handle only one kind of animal, so farms like Clark Summit have to cart their pigs across the state. And USDA slaughter is costly. But it's all doable, the Clark Summit folks say. Response from their customers keeps Liz and Dan going. In fact, they've had trouble recently keeping up with demand—which bodes well for the renaissance of sustainable, local meats.

Dan got a call recently from a woman in Texas who had heard about the farm and wanted to buy Clark Summit meat. He kindly advised her to buy close to home. —Carol Ness

Dan waters the pigs as cattle graze on the range.

PREVIOUS PAGE: *Laying hens peck for worms and bugs.*

Vang and Moua Family Farms
FARMING IN A NEW WORLD

Subsistence farming, or living entirely off what you produce yourself, has a rich history in North America as elsewhere, but it's the rare grower or community that practices it today. When stories of subsistence farming do surface, they tend to be attached to journalistic or off-the-grid experiments (as in, Is it actually still possible?) or religious beliefs (as with the Amish). And then there are the Hmong immigrants from Laos, for whom subsistence farming was a kind of secular religion back home in the mountainous region bordering on China, and for whom this way of life remains a near and cherished memory. The greatest concentration of Laotian Hmong farmers in America—about 1,500— live in the Fresno area, combining the old ways with an entrepreneurialism that creates

Though he isn't there yet, Va Moua's dream is to farm organically.

opportunities but also reveals the harsh realities of operating at the margins of a new world.

Chao Vang and Xia Thao have farmed for 25 years in Fresno, raising 10 children and building a successful market for their enormous variety of produce. "Back home we grew and raised everything we ate, from the crops to the chickens and pigs and doves and pigeons," says Chao. "You couldn't have sold your soybeans even if you'd wanted to, because all your neighbors grew their own. There was no such thing as commercial farming. Now, we make food for others—but also for ourselves, as much as we can."

Back home, too, you laid claim to a plot of land and farmed it till you were ready to move on. The American system of land ownership is a new, and often exclusionary, challenge for Hmong farmers in California, and soaring prices are just part of the problem. A farmer

with years or even decades of experience may lack the required credit history. And while Hmong farmers grow the very definition of specialty products—harvests with built-in demand that are not available through mainstream channels such as supermarkets—many lenders have never heard of the crops they grow nor imagined that so many different ones could be profitably grown together. For the Hmong, the idea that farming one or two crops over and over again would be advantageous is just one of the many oddities of the conventional American farming system.

The Vangs lease small parcels of land, currently farming about 8 acres. Walking (and munching) through the farm, you come across corn, *kabocha,* chayote, carrots, *sin qua,* pigeon peas, amaranth, nightshade, multiple varieties of tomatoes and beans, lemongrass, cilantro, peanuts, chilies, sweet-potato leaf, okra leaf, bitter melon, sour leaf, cucumbers, and sweet and Thai and Vietnamese basil. That's a partial list. "We grow Filipino eggplant and Japanese eggplant and Italian eggplant and Indian eggplant and also Chinese eggplant," Chao says. "There is no Hmong eggplant—we can share the Chinese one!"

Commercial farming methods have overtaken traditional techniques, so that organic fertilizing and field rotation have given way to buying chemicals and seeds, and abandoning a leasehold when the land depletes. In fact,

organic, which was for centuries simply the norm, is now a luxury the Vangs consider beyond reach, given the rising price of organic fertilizers and the red tape involved in certification. (Conversion to organic on leased land adds a few more rolls of tape.)

As for so many small farms, the enterprise hinges on finding a way to sell directly to consumers. Local warehouses and other wholesalers will buy, "but they will pay nothing," says a local farm extension agent who works with the Hmong community. The Vangs have found their niche: the Cerritos Farmers' Market, a few miles northwest of Long Beach, where they sell every Saturday for most of the year. Don't miss the sour leaf; Xia shows you how to eat it fresh-picked, sprinkled with a little salt and chili. "Very good on a hot day," she says.

The Mouas, a few miles down the road from the Vangs, are the rare and fortunate family whose oldest member, Michael, owns the land. His younger brother, Va, emerges from under a huge tree to welcome visitors. Its branches form a cavernous room where Va's wife, Cindy, and sister-in-law are washing greens in a big

---

The blazing Fresno heat calls for ingenious shade solutions.
PREVIOUS PAGE: *Xia Thao and her husband, Chao Vang, at their farm.*

wooden tub and other family members are heating tea, finishing lunch, and making bunches of produce. To be invited in from the 100-degree heat to this shady enclosure feels like stepping into another world—spray from the water hose hangs suspended in the air, and you hear the soft, continuous slap of greens being swooshed through the tub. Just-picked and luscious, many with flowers and vegetable buds attached, they're laid end to end in glistening piles. "There are many names for what we grow," says Va, pointing to one pile. "You can call this *tong choi,* or Chinese spinach, or water spinach, or," he smiles, "perhaps something else. The names are not so important to Asian customers. What's important is that they can find all the produce that is familiar and all the different things they want. The markets in Asia have much more variety than Americans are used to."

The Mouas sell at two farmers' markets, one in South San Francisco and the other in Concord, in the East Bay. Their bunches of greens are dispatched by the hundreds—*tong choi* (we'll call it) and chili leaves, bitter melon and okra leaf, dill and many different basils, to name a few. Va, a "part-time" farmer who also runs a travel business in town, made a bet a couple of years ago on the jujube, a small, fruit-bearing tree. He says the fruit's taste reminds some people of an apple, then shakes his head slightly as if to suggest that it's a sadly crude comparison. Dried jujubes are sweet, almost candylike orbs. Some people make medicinal tea from the jujube, and in parts of Asia it's considered a Cupid's arrow as well as a harbinger of fertility. For Va, it was enterprise agriculture: The per-pound price was high, and the growing conditions auspicious. Four years later, a glut of production has driven the price way down, and he's not sure if he's going to be a jujube grower after all. "Farming is very old work," he says, "and always new."—Katrina Heron

Michael Moua at the family farm. PREVIOUS PAGE: *A giant tree shields and shades the produce prep area.*

Instantly Artisan

Not exactly shortcuts—more like taste tricks

Frozen Pops
Measure 4 cups of a fresh ripe fruit and put into a food processor or blender. Puree or mash until the fruit becomes liquid. Add a tablespoon or two of sugar. Transfer the mixture into frozen-pop molds and freeze.

Yogurt Cheese
Pour 2 quarts of plain yogurt into a colander lined with a clean dish towel or a few layers of cheesecloth. Place the colander on a bowl and allow the yogurt to drain overnight in the fridge. The next day, mix in some salt and enjoy on toast or slices of fresh tomato.

Fast Refrigerator Apricot Jam
Combine 3 cups of fresh ripe pitted apricots with a cup of sugar in a pan. Bring to a boil, mashing the mixture as it cooks. Boil, stirring frequently, for 10 minutes and add a tablespoon of butter and a tablespoon of lemon juice. Allow to cool, then store in the fridge in a covered bowl or Tupperware container.

Honey and Nuts
Mix 2 cups of honey and 1 cup of fresh walnuts and almonds in a bowl. The nuts can be roughly chopped or left whole. Serve on buttered toast or warm up and drizzle on ice cream.

Refrigerator Pickles
Wash and scrub 3 large cucumbers. Leaving the skin on, slice them into $1/8$-inch slices into a bowl. Remove the seeds from a bell pepper and the skin from an onion and finely chop both before adding to the cucumbers. Sprinkle the mix with a tablespoon of salt and 2 teaspoons of celery seed. Cover and set aside for an hour. In a small saucepan, bring $1/2$ cup of vinegar to a boil, then remove immediately from the heat. Stir in 4 tablespoons of sugar until dissolved. Allow to cool, then pour over the cucumbers. Wait a full day before serving. These pickles will last up to 3 weeks in the fridge.

Pixie Growers
A TANGERINE LOVE STORY

VENTURA COUNTY

Wrapped in the thin, easy-to-peel skin of the Pixie tangerine is a farm story as sweet and bright as the fruit itself. It starts with two little farm kids, Emily Thacher and her brother, George, hanging around the Friend's Ranches packinghouse in the California citrus paradise that is the Ojai Valley, while their parents and grandparents sorted and boxed Valencia oranges and Dancy tangerines.

It was the late 1970s, and Jim Churchill was scouting for something to plant in his orchard to replace the Bacon avocados his father had put in but no one wanted anymore. Valencia oranges, Ojai's mainstay, were no longer an option, since the seedless navel oranges had eclipsed them. Jim stopped by Friend's, peeled a

random tangerine, scarfed it down, and asked Emily's father, Tony Thacher, something like, "What's that? And why don't you sell it?"

"That," said Tony, "is the Pixie." But Friend's had only a few trees, so while Tony packed the earlier varieties, the kids would eat all the Pixies. It was an "aha" moment for Jim, who thought, "Sweet, easy to peel, and seedless? Kids love it? I can sell it."

In that moment, a future was born for the Thachers; for Jim and his wife and cofarmer, Lisa Brenneis; for their farms—and for the Pixie tangerine itself. In the homogenization of the modern American produce marketplace, the Pixie was fast disappearing. It had been developed by University of California researchers in 1927 and earned a reputation for its flavor and ease of eating. But it didn't ripen till April or May, when supermarkets were switching from citrus to strawberries and cherries.

The Pixie Growers Association gave the tangerine a recognizable label.

Ojai, with its midday heat and evening cool, had just the right climate for the Pixie. It's like *terroir* and wine grapes, says Emily: Place delivers an indelible quality. So the Thachers and the Churchill Orchard duo set about making a name—and a place in the market—for the Ojai Pixie. Along with a few other tangerine growers, they formed the Ojai Pixie Growers Association, a loosely organized group that shares growing tips and marketing. "We thought, 'Why don't we see if we can work together instead of cannibalizing each other?'" says Jim. "It's like a users' group for tangerines."

The story could end here, with the happy news that the plan worked, the Pixies were brought back from the edge, and the Churchill and Thacher farms tootled happily into their future. All that is true. But it's also a richer tale, and its details offer insights into just how hard it can be to achieve the dream of a sustainable and local food system in America, and why farming can keep Emily Thacher up at night.

First off, none of these growers ever intended to be farmers. Not Jim Churchill and Lisa Brenneis. Not Tony and Anne Thacher, and not their daughter, Emily.

Jim's father planted his avocado orchard as a tax dodge in the 1970s. (He ran an educational

film company in Los Angeles.) But Jim came to love Ojai from the 5 years the family lived there when he was a boy. When his big-city community organizing work ran out in 1978, he headed south to run the ranch. Romance brought in Lisa, who was—and is—a filmmaker; she and Jim met when she worked for Jim's father, and it took years before the farm was earning enough to let her move to Ojai full-time.

Disaster is what turned Tony and Anne Thacher into farmers—that and Anne's deep connection to the orchards. Her grandfather, William Friend, planted them. Her father, George Elmer Friend, spent his lifetime farming them. And Anne grew up in them. Tony Thacher jokes that he married the farmer's daughter, and it's not really a joke; he came from a family of educators whose name is on one of Ojai's oldest private schools.

In 1969, Tony was working toward a PhD in geology at UC Berkeley and Anne was teaching chemistry at San Francisco State when an epic flood destroyed the Friend's Ranches packinghouse and farmstead. A call for help went out. Tony and Anne headed back to the farm, and they never left.

Emily remembers that when she went away to college, the fragrance of citrus blossoms pulled her back to the farm every April. She studied biology and taught sustainable development in Costa Rica before catching the agroecology

Jim Churchill, framed by the groves of Friend's Ranches.

81

bug and heading back to school for a master's in pest management. Now, she runs the farm with her parents and lives amid citrus groves where she and husband Tony Ayala, a US Forest Service fire battalion chief, are raising the first of the next generation, 1-year-old Oliver.

Once the Pixie Growers Association was up and running, the members learned how difficult it was going to be to sell the fruit. Supermarkets didn't want them, for several reasons. They're small and hard to stack. The supply was relatively tiny. And Pixies ripen at the tail end of the long tangerine season, when consumers are supposedly hungry for something new. "Then I found Bill," Jim says. Bill Fujimoto, who runs the legendary Monterey Market in Berkeley, agreed to try them. Jim put two boxes on a Greyhound bus north the next day. The Pixie was on its way.

Bill, who seeks out the best and most interesting fruits and vegetables even if he can't always make much money on them, bought Jim Churchill's entire crop of Pixies for 8 years. "He made the market," says Jim. Fujimoto has done the same for many other small farmers, prompting Lisa to make a film about him, *Eat at Bill's*. Slow Food USA has added the Pixie to its Ark of Taste, a catalog of endangered edibles that deserve to be rescued. Eventually, Jim and Friend's were growing too many Pixies for Monterey Market—but not enough to segue neatly into the wholesale world. Jim went back out to sell, this time with some confidence and a success story to tell.

One specialty wholesaler wanted to change the Pixie's name. Another wanted only the large fruit. Finally, Jim found Melissa's in Los Angeles, the rare wholesaler willing to aggregate small quantities from several farmers and pay the premium that Ojai fruit commanded.

Since then, the Pixie's success has prompted other growers to pile on: 20,000 acres of Pixies have been planted in the Ojai Valley since 2000, Emily says. That could send the price into a death spiral. Along with recent, drastic increases in the prices of fertilizer, fuel, water, and labor, not to mention land— "well, that's what I have nightmares about," she adds.

Even so, these farmers wouldn't do anything else. You can see it in Emily's face as she invites visitors back for the spring bloom. "It's like your own little pirate ship," says Lisa. Adds Jim, "It's not an economically rational pursuit," but there's a rare satisfaction that comes from being part of a revolution in how food is grown and sold. "And we've got a front-row seat."—Carol Ness

One-year-old Oliver likes oranges, as befits a fourth-generation citrus kid.

83

J&P Organics
A FAMILY SUCCESS STORY

MONTEREY COUNTY

The *P* of J&P Organics is Pablo Perez. Pablo, with his callused ham-hock hands, ruddy face, and battered panama hat, looks like a campesino called in from central casting. The *J* stands for Juan Perez—Pablo's son. In contrast to his father's old-world style, Juan favors a look that marks him as a definitive product of the USA: aggressive black sunglasses with fluorescent orange pads, artfully darned jeans, a neatly trimmed goatee, hair that's buzzed to the scalp on the sides and gelled over on top.

Pablo is in charge of the land—the hoeing, planting, and harvesting. Juan is responsible for the marketing, the bookkeeping, and the talking. He's especially well suited for this last duty. His cellphone buzzes every few minutes,

Pablo and Juan Perez on the five acres they farm.

and he shifts effortlessly from speaking Spanish with his parents to answering customers' questions in flawless English.

"J&P Organics. Yes, we deliver right to your house. No, I can just leave it by your front door if you're at work. Hello, J&P Organics. Rainbow chard? Yeah it's great, we're just eating some now. Well, normally you cook it, but you can eat it raw. If you don't want it, you can just make a note on the form and I'll replace it with something else."

When he talks about his farm, Juan Perez will interrupt his own stream of speech with mile-long lists, ticking off his fingers: "Right now we are growing strawberries, raspberries, corn, squash, zucchini, red onions, white onions, cilantro . . ."

List-making farmers are a rarity these days. Ask a farmer what he grows and you may well

85

get a one-word answer. Juan and Pablo's neighbors around Salinas might say simply, "Artichokes" or "Salad greens." Examine these monocultural farms and you'll find row after row of identical green sprigs emerging at regular intervals from otherwise bare earth. These fields have a certain industrial beauty—they represent a triumph of human control over the chaotic abundance of plant life—but there's not much to see there beyond the first glance. Every square foot of J&P Organics, on the other hand, is packed with diversity.

" . . . beets, carrots, celery, peppers, acorn squash, butternut squash, what's that other winter squash? Um, pumpkins . . . "

Pablo and his wife, Florencia, came to California from Ciudad de Insurgentes, a small farming town in Baja California, Mexico, a few hours north of La Paz. Like many immigrants, they had worked as farm laborers, but in 1997 they raised enough money to lease 5 acres of land and began farming for themselves. They planted raspberries and flowers. For this initial foray into working for themselves, the family didn't consider going organic—they purchased fertilizers and pesticides to insure their investment. That worked fine until the pump that supplied water to the land broke. The landlord refused to fix the machinery, and without irrigation, the plants withered.

When Juan went to Cal State Monterey Bay, he was intent on creating better opportunities for himself so that he wouldn't have to work in the fields. He flirted with the humanities and took classes in computer science and business before fixing on a concentration in science. In his science classes, he learned about agricultural chemicals running off into the ocean and seeping into workers' skin. And it was in the science department that he saw a flyer posted on the wall advertising a paid summer internship on an organic farm. Even though he'd meant to get away from farming, he figured he'd benefit more from an agricultural internship than from spending another summer working on the Santa Cruz beach boardwalk. The internship was at the Agriculture and Land-Based Training Association (ALBA), which offers programs to help small organic farmers get started. After spending two summers learning about farming and marketing, Juan asked his father to take a class with him at ALBA.

"I went to school to get a better job, and it brought me back to farming," Juan says. "I guess it's in my blood, or it's destiny or something."

The father-and-son team started by providing vegetables to five students. Now

A riot of flowers grows alongside the vegetables at J&P.

they lease five acres from ALBA and deliver to more than 100 customers ("in Del Monte, Seaside, Carmel, Moss Landing, Santa Cruz, Dominican Hospital, Monterey Bay Aquarium, Pacific Grove, Watsonville, Pebble Beach . . ."). Five acres isn't much, but the land is providing enough income to support the family. Pablo was able to quit his job as a building manager, and now he's living his dream: growing food and working for himself. "He's wanted to be a farmer ever since he was a little boy, and he works—" Juan lifts his eyebrows, "a lot. I'll call him on a Sunday and he'll be over there, driving the tractor."

At home in Watsonville, where Juan lives with his parents and siblings, there are iconlike paintings of the Madonna and saints on the walls and lace curtains on the windows. Peeling linoleum under the refrigerator reveals another layer of flooring from years past. Both are scrubbed immaculately clean. Florencia rules the kitchen, chopping chard and zucchini from the farm on a folding table by the window. The family isn't working with a lot of extra money, but they are making a living off the land. Recently, they were able to buy their own tractor. Not a gleaming new, house-size piece of machinery with a GPS-linked automatic driving device—it's a battered old harvester. Still, that's exactly what they need to get the job done. The cost of running a small organic farm has been within the Perezes' means, while large-scale monoculture growing would have been beyond reach, had they even wished to pursue it. As farms have gotten bigger, the gap between owner and laborer has widened correspondingly, making it more difficult for immigrant workers to leap the divide. As a result, an economic hierarchy has developed along racial lines: White farmers own the land and brown laborers work it. Innovators like Juan and Pablo are adding some variety to that dichromatic separation.

When the pair show off their handiwork to visitors, they quickly fall into their respective roles: Juan picking sugary, plump strawberries to sample while Pablo drifts off with a hoe to attend to a weedy row. The field is jammed with a riotous profusion of plants, not just Juan's never-ending list of vegetables, but flowers as well. The mixture encourages beneficial insects, and, Juan says, "It's just more interesting to have variety. These are irises. And dahlias. We have gladiolas, strawflowers, yarrow, sunflowers, statices. . . ."
—Nathanael Johnson

Pablo, hoeing the rows, is rarely away from the farm.

How-To: Green Kitchen

5 Great Tools

Indispensable, widely available, and eminently practical

Mortar and Pestle

WHAT IT IS A heavy bowl (mortar) and a thick baton (pestle) made from stone or clay, used to crush substances.

WHY IT'S GREAT Makes it easy to use fresh herbs to brighten up simple cooked dishes; good for making your own marinades and herb mixes. Also a wonderful way to get guests at your home involved in helping out.

WHY IT'S GREEN Helps you use more fresh ingredients easily and never needs to be replaced.

Cast-Iron Pot

WHAT IT IS A Dutch oven made of solid cast iron.

WHY IT'S GREAT Perfect for cooking inexpensive braised meats, frying eggs, and preparing fresh tomato sauce.

WHY IT'S GREEN Lasts forever.

Food Dehydrator

WHAT IT IS A solar- or electric-powered contraption that dries produce.

WHY IT'S GREAT Lets you preserve fruits, vegetables, and herbs in quantity for months to come.

WHY IT'S GREEN Helps you extend your enjoyment of local produce, eating out of season from your own stores.

Herb Pot

WHAT IT IS A pot of soil you keep on the counter to grow a few of your favorite herbs from seed.

WHY IT'S GREAT Keeps herbs handy—no need to run to the store when you're missing that crucial sprig of thyme. Encourages you to cook more and perfumes your kitchen.

WHY IT'S GREEN None of those plastic herb packs.

Terra-Cotta Crock

WHAT IT IS A pot made from clay.

WHY IT'S GREAT Perfect for cooking beans, stews, and more in the oven—try loading it up with herbs, broth, wine, and some dry beans and leaving it in the oven overnight at the lowest setting. Make sure to keep it covered; if your crock doesn't have a lid, borrow the one that goes with your Dutch oven or use a ceramic plate as a cover.

WHY IT'S GREEN Goes from oven to fridge—no need for multiple containers—and is made from sustainable, low-environmental-impact materials.

Redwood Roots Farm

THE CIRCLE OF SUPPORT

HUMBOLDT COUNTY

J anet Czarnecki signs the newsletter she sends to members of her Redwood Roots Farm's CSA "Love, your farmer, Janet."

She means it—both the "love" and the "your." On her tiny, precisely planted patch—just 4 acres in a narrow valley close by the northern California coastal town of Arcata—this ebullient mother hen of a farmer has sown the idea of community at the very core of her operation.

Her members, or shareholders, are essentially cofarmers and family who bring the kids and the cousins out to gather and pick, or take their dogs down to the creek; who study farm insects or pruning at the farm's workshop;

Thanks to the farm, whose fenced fields run along the right side of the lane, Jacoby Creek Valley has kept its rural character.

who pitch in when the water pump fails or the classroom needs some paint. Interns and volunteers are attracted like aphids to spring roses and end up working for years.

In Janet's world, community *is* sustainability—along with long days of back-straining labor. Her approach is one model for the back-to-the-future small-farm economy in America. "We have created a circle of mutual support," is the way she puts it. "The theoretical framework behind the Community Supported Agriculture concept comes to life!"

The circle is in full view any day of the week at Redwood Roots Farm, in the Jacoby Creek Valley. It's right next door to a shiny new two-garage home—a reminder of what almost happened to the fertile floodplain acreage now occupied by the farm. In the 1980s, the owners became concerned about the way development was gobbling up farmland and placed 10 creekside acres in a conservation easement. On 6 acres, the creek and wildlife habitat have been restored; Redwood Roots Farm occupies the rest. The original owners still live across the road.

The community feel is immediate: The Unitarian Universalist Fellowship, next door to the farm, shares its parking lot with Redwood Roots visitors. It's just a short stroll down a dirt lane to the farm's cluster of open sheds, plus a gaily painted one-room workshop/classroom. There's no barn or farmhouse, in accordance with the conservation easement rules; Janet lives in town.

In one shed, out of the sun's glare if not the heat, Amanda Beatty is washing, drying, and bundling bright bunches of tender white turnips for the next day's farmers' market and member "share day," the day the members come out to pick up their produce. It's Amanda's fifth season on the crew, as she's completed her master's degree at nearby Humboldt State in the globalization of agriculture.

In the kitchen lean-to, Erin Derden-Little sautés green garlic on a two-burner stovetop. She's making the crew's lunch from lettuces, asparagus, snap peas, and turnips, augmented by shiitakes, dried beans, and barley from local farms. Sun-hot strawberries make up dessert. Erin runs the farm's program of workshops, classes, and school visits. It's her third year at Redwood Roots, after navigating Cornell and a master's in international agriculture development. She's more confident talking about commodities than cooking, but today is her day in the lunch rotation.

Out in the fields, rows of new onion starts are wilting under Janet's anxious eye. Just 4 miles from the Pacific and hemmed in by forested mountains rising to the Coastal Range, the valley tends to have cooler weather. But the day dawned to a rare scorcher—and there's no irrigation. The pump quit 4 days earlier. It's a big problem for a small farm. A new pump costs $7,000, and Redwood Roots, while earning Janet and her crew a bare living, doesn't have money in the bank. "I asked the pump guy to come out, with no idea how I was going to pay him," she says. A quick stop by a shareholder's home solves the problem. A loan is promised. The water should be back on in time to save the onions.

Janet's landlords, Wilma and Howard, helped her buy her land. (Howard died last year at 97, and a big, comfy, handmade bench in his memory faces the grassy area where kids play with hula hoops on share day. His ashes were scattered around it.) Between the crew, volunteers, and shareholders, Janet says, "There's so much interest and care in the farm—that contributes to its sustainability."

Janet samples lunch in the open-air shed.

As devoted as she is to the farm's theoretical framework, Janet does this work for one reason: "I love to farm." As a student at the University of Michigan in the 1970s, she escaped the classroom to cultivate a plot in the Ann Arbor community garden. Later, after working in agroecology and farm gardens in California, she returned to Michigan in the late 1980s to help start one of the nation's pioneering CSAs, the Community Farm of Ann Arbor, which thrives today. Redwood Roots Farm got its start in 1998. Janet joined the operation a year later and has been sole proprietor since 2002.

She tells her story over lunch, with her crew, volunteers, and visitors gathered in the farm's largest shed, where shareholders come every Tuesday and Friday afternoon to pick up their weekly fruits and vegetables, paying on a sliding scale of $400 to $500 for a 20-week season. Instead of receiving the boxed deliveries more common in cities, Redwood Roots members come out and pack their own. A whiteboard tells them how many bunches of turnips or baskets of berries are theirs; if they don't want the kohlrabi, they don't take any. Moms bring their kids for picnics. Families come to special "U-pick" days. It's a resource and creates community

just as farmers' markets do in cities. "People start calling it their farm," Erin says.

The shed is broiling, even in the shade, and everyone's been working since early morning. Taj and Skeezer, the Redwood Roots dogs, loll in cooler corners. Passing the bean-and-barley stew, the crew make it clear that, like Janet, they're motivated both by a love of farming and by a belief that small, local community farms hold the prospect of a better future for the world and for them. Sharing the daily gleanings at a long picnic table feels almost sacred.

Eddie Tanner, the third crew member, who graduated from Humboldt State with a degree in soil science, is looking for land nearby to start his own CSA. He has the name picked out—Deep Seeded Community Farm—and knows the operation will be based on the Redwood Roots model: close to town, with lots of community involvement.

His farm will be a little bigger, though—an economic decision based on his plan to distribute his harvests more widely. Four acres works for Janet, partly because she sells directly to consumers, and also because it's a scale she can manage herself. "I know all the shareholders' names and their kids' names and their mothers' names and their roommates' names," she says. And everyone, even the littlest, knows hers.—Carol Ness

Mirabai Collins, a farm intern, rinses fruit in the outdoor kitchen sink.
PREVIOUS PAGE: China Rose garlic is laid out to cure.

Land for Sale

EVERY HOUR, SPRAWL EATS UP 125 ACRES of America's fast-dwindling farmland. That's 2 acres every minute, or 750 farms the size of Redwood Roots every day. § This estimate comes from an oft-quoted study by the American Farmland Trust (AFT), which exists to try to stanch the loss. The figures don't take into account the number of new, small farms blooming as part of the modern-day drive toward sustainability, but the decades-long trend would be hard to reverse entirely: Big farms have swallowed small ones, and the number of American farmers has steadily plummeted. § The reasons are well-known: Small farms have a hard time making money, as have many larger farms until the recent surge in commodity prices. § Population growth—100 million new Americans are predicted by 2040—is another reason farmland is disappearing. And so is shortsighted or simply bad development planning, according to the AFT study. From 1982 to 1997, the US population grew 17 percent, while the amount of land consumed by development increased almost three times as much: 47 percent. More and more people, the study showed, want to live large, on 10-acre plots—big enough for a small farm.

Selling the farm is often a farmer's only financial option. But there are many good arguments for saving farms. Among them:

- ✓ Keeping small local farms near urban areas means fresher fruits and vegetables for city dwellers, and that's healthy for both. And farms provide leafy, green oases amid freeways and buildings.

- ✓ Visiting farms and getting to know farmers helps reconnect people with the land and shortens the distance between food producers and what's on our plates.

- ✓ Well-managed farms can help protect the environment by preventing soil erosion, keeping pesticides and fertilizers out of air and streams, and giving wild creatures places to live.

- ✓ If farms are local, food doesn't have to travel so far, reducing the energy consumed and greenhouse gases generated between field and table.

- ✓ Local food, picked riper and delivered faster, simply tastes better.

Tierra Miguel Farm
ANNALS OF LAND CONSERVATION

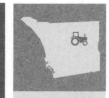

SAN DIEGO COUNTY

The Tierra Miguel Farm stretches out over 85 acres on the wide floodplain of a valley so classically picturesque it reminds many visitors of Tuscany in a Renaissance painting. Only about an hour's drive north of San Diego, the landscape feels removed from modern-day concerns, as if stashed in a verdant antiquity. Like a lot of things about the place, this turns out to be true, in a way.

A large swath of the pristine Pauma Valley belongs to the reservations of several Luiseño tribes, among them the Pauma Band of Mission Indians. The main road here is flanked by citrus orchards extending to the foothills, where avocados take over; they climb up the mountainsides to jagged peaks ringing the valley. Tierra Miguel Farm is a lone patchwork of row crops on the valley floor, with a small stone-fruit orchard of its own, a wood-framed yellow farmhouse, a big barn, some outbuildings, a trailer, and, near the roadside, a produce stand with a sign explaining that payment is on the honor system. For sale year-round, depending on the season: all kinds of greens, broccoli, cabbages, herbs, rhubarb, berries, carrots, flowers, squash, beets, eggplant, and tomatoes.

The Tierra Miguel story begins in 1999, when the proprietor of this lowland oasis, an organic strawberry farmer, decided to cash in his chips (corny but irresistible—four casinos are a stone's throw away). He agreed to lease the land to an eager new band of growers—not exactly farmers, and not exactly a family— who were determined to prove by example the ongoing viability of small farming and

Milijan Krecu, Tierra Miguel's farm manager leads students on a tour (center). A gathering of foundation volunteers (lower right).

103

biodynamic practices in the region. Not far north, over the line into Los Angeles and Orange counties, almost all the small farms had already been lost to real estate development. This group of close friends had hatched the revolutionary idea of creating a nonprofit farm and CSA that would partner with the valley community as a food provider and restore the hope (and the memory) of fresh local produce to greater Los Angeles. Over time, they also hoped to further the practice of biodynamic farming, and to help organize a network of small sustainable farms that would lead to larger markets and new supporters.

They named their 501(c)(3) the Tierra Miguel Foundation. They had organization and management expertise in a variety of professions, optimism, farming know-how, and funding, in roughly descending order. The first serious challenge arose in 2003, when the strawberry-farmer-turned-landlord was offered about $2 million by a developer seeking home sites for a country club and golf course that (invisibly, it must be said) abuts the property. "We realized we needed to find a way to buy the land," says Beth Ann Levendoski, one of the foundation's founders and its director. The farm's CSA and internship programs were off and running, along with its outreach to educational institutions (from the local elementary school to the Los Angeles Unified School District to various universities) and its partnership with health organizations such as the Indian Health Clinic. Yet all of this, even the farm's festivals, was suddenly eclipsed by the urgent need to preserve the land itself. Led by Beth Ann, the group approached the California Department of Conservation, which had recently launched the California Farmland Conservancy Program (CFCP), hoping to secure funding to rescue the land from development. "We invited them down to look at the farm," she says. The officials came, saw, and agreed that the property qualified.

Pooling resources from a number of state and federal agencies and programs, Tierra Miguel obtained financing to purchase an agricultural conservation easement from the landowner; the easement forever prohibits practices that would damage or interfere with the agricultural use of the land. "We were the first California agricultural easement placed anywhere south of Santa Barbara," Beth Ann says proudly. It was a landmark event, not least in highlighting new resources for preserving the area's farmsteads. "There's this perception that farming south of the Central Valley is nonexistent," she says. "But in fact, San Diego County has the largest number of small farms in the nation. The question is how to keep them intact."

Scoring another first in California, the foundation was soon awarded a temporary fee title grant, whereby it was granted funding to purchase the land outright, provided it would soon sell the land into private ownership and return the proceeds from the sale to the CFCP. The group now had 3 years in which to find a private buyer who wanted a working farm with a conservation easement attached. With any luck, this new owner would also be interested in leasing the land back to the Tierra Miguel Foundation.

No takers—until, to their surprise, the Pauma Band of Mission Indians came calling. They were neighbors, which was good, but as members of a sovereign nation, they weren't bound to land-use rules conceived in American law, which was problematic. And then, yet another first.

"The Pauma Band have a history as orchardists, and they've been involved in reforesting the mountains behind their reservation," Beth Ann says. "When we all met as a group, the Pauma chairman, Chris Devers, said, 'This is our valley. We want to honor the easement as a statement of our commitment to the land.' There wasn't a dry eye in the house." The sale was completed soon after.

With the future secure (the foundation has a 10-year lease with an option to renew), the farm is back in business, as it were, gearing up its CSA and redoubling its efforts in health-care and educational outreach. Milijan Krecu, a founding board member and the farm manager for most of the past decade, can once again focus on building a small-farm network.

And on farming. Mil has plans to take seeds from one of Tierra Miguel's most prized melons, the amazingly perfumy Rayyan, and back-breed them (take the seed out of a hybridized form and into a more stable, open-pollinated one). He also has a new idea about greenhousing (phase it out and direct-seed instead), a new source for plant stakes (locust trees, which he is planting on the farm), and a hunch about why the sandy soil near the valley bottom isn't retaining nutrients as he had hoped. "The mistakes are always great teachers," he says. He is philosophical, too, about the trials of the past few years. "We set precedents with the IRS—they had never heard of a 501(c)(3) CSA before—and I don't really recommend that to anybody," he says with a laugh. Then he goes on more seriously: "We want to keep working in the context of community. It's our basic belief system, and why we started the foundation in the first place. We didn't want this farm to be *ours*. It should, in the greater sense, belong to the community, to the world. We're caretaking for the time being."—Katrina Heron

Recipes

Paul's Best Biscuit Recipe

SWEET HOME RANCH

2 cups all-purpose unbleached flour
1½ tablespoons baking powder
½ teaspoon baking soda
½ teaspoon salt
⅓ cup unsalted butter, frozen
1¼ cup buttermilk with 2% butterfat content (or 1 cup buttermilk with 1% butterfat content)

Preheat the oven to 450°F. Blend the flour, baking powder, baking soda, and salt. Cut the frozen butter into small bits and blend into the flour mixture with a pastry cutter or two sharp knives. Add the buttermilk and mix.

On a floured surface, flatten the dough to about 1" thick, then fold in half. Do this three times quickly, but no more. Flatten the dough to ¾" thick. Cut into 3 rounds with a sharp, clean, floured biscuit cutter. Press down straight and quickly; do not twist. Pull up and place the biscuit on a cookie sheet. Clean any dough from the cutter, press into the bowl of flour, and cut another biscuit. Continue until all the dough is used.

Bake until golden, about 10 minutes. Serve hot, with jam.

Makes 12 biscuits

Whole Wheat Biscuits

BURROUGHS FAMILY FARMS

2 cups whole wheat flour (or 1 cup whole wheat and 1 cup all-purpose flour)
2 teaspoons double-acting baking powder
½ teaspoon baking soda
2 teaspoons sugar
¾ teaspoon salt
⅓ cup cold butter
1 cup buttermilk or kefir

Preheat the oven to 400°F.

Mix the flour, baking powder, baking soda, sugar, and salt in a bowl, then cut in the butter with a pastry blender. When the mixture has a fine-crumb consistency, use a fork to stir in the buttermilk or kefir. Place on a floured board and knead gently and quickly—about eight folds. Roll out and cut or simply shape with your hands. Place on an ungreased baking sheet and bake for 12 to 15 minutes, until lightly browned. Serve with lots of butter and honey or jam.

Makes 10 to 12 large biscuits

Whole Wheat Flat Bread

WINDBORNE FARM

Jennifer makes her bread using desem *starter, but the recipe below, inspired by hers, has been modified to use regular yeast. The long, slow fermentation process of desem naturally enhances the nuttiness of whole wheat flour, creating a more complex flavor in the flat breads than can be achieved with regular yeast. However, making desem is extremely complex. The short version: Take a small amount of freshly milled whole wheat flour, mix it with water, then bury it in an additional 10 pounds of freshly milled whole wheat flour. After about a week, the starter naturally ferments and can be broken open and used to leaven fresh flour. If you're interested, seek out all the details online or in a specialty bread-baking book.*

**1¹⁄₂ cups whole wheat flour
1 package quick-rising yeast
³⁄₄ teaspoon salt
¹⁄₂ to ²⁄₃ cup hot water (120° to 130°F)
2 teaspoons extra-virgin olive oil**

Preheat the oven to 500°F or the highest setting. Place a pizza stone or inverted baking sheet on the lowest oven rack.

Combine the flour, yeast, and salt in a large mixing bowl, and mix the hot water and oil in a measuring cup. Slowly add the hot-water mixture to the flour mixture. Mix with a wooden spoon until the ingredients are blended, then turn out onto a lightly floured surface and knead for 5 minutes. Cover the dough with a damp kitchen towel and let it rest for at least 20 minutes. Cut the dough into 2 pieces and roll each piece as thin as possible. Using a metal spatula or a pizza peel, lay each round of dough on the baking sheet or pizza stone and bake until the top is puffy and a few brown blisters appear. Eat immediately.

Makes 2 flat breads

Warm Fava Bean Salad

FULL BELLY FARM

Judith uses an unusual technique to prepare her fava beans—boiling them whole in their shells. The salad she makes with the cooked beans is liberally seasoned with butter and herbs.

30 large fava beans
Salt
3 tablespoons butter
8 sage leaves, roughly chopped
Lemon juice (optional)

Bring an 8-quart pasta pot filled with water to a boil and add salt as you would for pasta. Drop the fava beans in and boil for 6 minutes. Drain the water from the beans and let them cool for 15 minutes. While the fava beans are cooling, warm the butter in a saucepan and add the sage leaves. Cook them over low heat for 5 minutes, or until you can smell the sage scent. When the beans have cooled, use your hands to squeeze the cooked beans out of the whole pods into a serving bowl. Dress the beans with the butter and fried sage. Season to taste with salt, pepper, and some lemon juice, if you like. Serve warm.

Makes 6 servings

Judith's Salad Dressing

FULL BELLY FARM

Judith made this salad dressing for robust red leaf lettuce at dinner on her farm. It could also be paired with spinach or arugula. The incredibly sweet, mild blue cheese she used was from a Vermont farm whose cheese maker is dating a Full Belly farmhand. A Maytag or Point Reyes blue would be a great option in this recipe.

½ cup olive oil
¼ teaspoon balsamic vinegar
2 teaspoons white wine vinegar
1 teaspoon salt
1 teaspoon dried oregano
½ cup blue cheese, roughly crumbled

Mix together all the ingredients with a fork. Dress the salad immediately before serving.

Makes 6 to 8 servings of dressed salad

Spearmint-Stuffed Artichokes

FULL BELLY FARM

The artichokes Judith uses for this dish are so fresh, the leaves snap off easily as you clean them. Look for the freshest artichokes by observing the cut stem— avoid artichokes with stems that are brown and soft.

8 sprigs spearmint
4 cloves garlic
2 tablespoons salt
8 small artichokes
1 cup olive oil

Chop the spearmint leaves, garlic, and salt together until they become a smooth paste, and divide into 8 portions.

Trim the artichokes by cutting off the top 1" with a serrated knife. Pull off and discard all the dark outer leaves, down to the pale yellow leaves with pale green tips. Cut ¼" from the end of the stem to expose the inner core. Trim the sides of the stem (leaving them attached) down to the pale inner core. If you're preparing the artichokes in advance, drop them in a quart of water with a whole lemon squeezed into it to keep the green color fresh. Using your finger or the handle of a wooden spoon, flatten the center of the artichoke, making a small concavity. Fill this hole with the mint mixture.

Pour the olive oil into a heavy-bottomed saucepan or terra-cotta pot and place the artichokes in it, choke-side down. Braise them, covered, at the lowest temperature possible for 1 hour. Remove from the stove and serve.

Makes 6 to 8 servings

Jennifer's Chickpea Puree

WINDBORNE FARM

2 cups dry chickpeas
10 cups water
Salt, lemon juice, freshly ground pepper, and olive oil to taste

Combine the chickpeas and water in a slow cooker or regular pot. If using a slow cooker, cook for 5 hours on high. In the oven, either leave the pot in the oven on the lowest possible temperature overnight, or cook for 5 hours at 350°F. Since the chickpeas are not soaked before cooking, you may find that the cooking time varies depending on their age. Make sure to taste for softness before pureeing.

Once they're cooked, strain the chickpeas, reserving the cooking liquid. Puree them with a few tablespoons of the cooking liquid until they're creamy and have no lumps. Salt to taste and add cooking liquid to the puree if you want the puree to be softer and more spreadable. If you like, add some lemon juice, pepper, and olive oil to taste.

Makes 8 servings (or 4 as a main course)

The Truth about Corn on the Cob Recipe

TAMAI FAMILY FARM

People have become accustomed to husking their corn before cooking it, but don't do it! A lot of the sugar is in the husk itself. To capture that flavor, soak picked corn in water for a few minutes. Then open the husk far enough that you can remove the silk. Refold the damp leaves over the cob. Roast the corn on a grill, turning frequently, then remove the husk and eat.

Fresh Black-Eyed Peas

WILL SCOTT JR.

Ham hocks and onions add seasoning to fresh black-eyed peas, a traditional Southern dish.

2 ham hocks
4 cups water, or as needed
4 cups fresh black-eyed peas, shelled
1 white onion, minced
Pinch of salt and freshly ground pepper

Place the ham hocks in a 4-quart Dutch oven or soup pan with water sufficient to cover them, and bring to a boil. Reduce the heat, cover, and simmer for 30 minutes. Add the peas, onion, and salt and pepper and cook for 40 minutes or so—until the peas are tender. Add more water if needed. If you like, cut up the meat from the hocks and add to the peas to serve.

Makes 6 servings

Stewed Greens

SLOW FOOD NATION KITCHEN

Mixed greens are perfect for this dish; anything goes, including turnip, mustard, and collard greens.

1½ gallons water
1 ham hock
2 dried red pepper pods
½ cup chopped white onion
1 tablespoon salt
2 pounds fresh greens
Cider vinegar to taste

In a large kettle, boil the water. Add the ham hock, red pepper, onion, and salt. Wash the greens thoroughly. Cut out the stems and cut the large leaves in strips. Add the greens to the boiling water, then cover and boil for about 1 hour. Allow the greens to cool slightly and serve with a splash of cider vinegar.

Makes 4 to 6 servings

Oven-Roasted Asparagus

FULL BELLY FARM

1 bunch (12 to 14 ounces) asparagus
4 tablespoons olive oil
1/2 teaspoon salt

Preheat the oven to 425°F. Trim off and discard the tough ends of the asparagus spears and lay the spears in a shallow ovenproof dish large enough to hold them in a double layer (12" round or 10" square). Jennifer makes hers in a 12" cast-iron skillet. Sprinkle the oil and salt over the asparagus and toss the spears to coat. Roast them until they're tender, about 15 minutes. When cooked, the asparagus will appear a little wrinkled, and their tips may brown.

For an extra indulgence, fry an egg and drape it over the cooked spears—using the yolk as dipping sauce—or sprinkle with 1/2 cup of grated hard cheese.

Makes 4 to 6 servings

Buttermilk Dressing

TIERRA MIGUEL FARM

2 cups buttermilk
1 whole hard-boiled egg
1/4 cup olive oil
10 sprigs parsley
5 sprigs celery leaves (optional)
2 cloves garlic
4 scallions, green and white parts chopped
1 handful of any fresh green herbs on hand, such as sorrel, nettle, watercress, or cilantro
Salt and freshly ground pepper to taste

Mix the buttermilk, egg, oil, parsley, celery leaves, garlic, scallions, and herbs in a blender or food processor until smooth. Add salt and pepper to taste.

Makes 6 to 8 servings of dressed salad

Medley of Roasted Vegetables with Balsamic Vinegar

TAMAI FAMILY FARM

Daisy Tamai, Jason's aunt, has been the family's designated head cook and recipe keeper for the past 30 years. "There's nothing better than a good home-cooked meal," she says. "It always seems to pull the family together, even through the most trying times."

2 medium-size green zucchini
2 medium-size gold zucchini
2 small Mexican squash (*chayote*)
2 large red bell peppers
2 large gold bell peppers
2 large green bell peppers
**2 bunches spring onions with nice-size bulbs
    (bulbs only)**
¼ cup balsamic vinegar
**¼ cup olive oil (enough to coat all the
    vegetables)**
Salt and freshly ground pepper to taste

Preheat oven to 400°F. Wash and cut all the vegetables into ½" pieces. Line a large baking sheet with foil or parchment paper and spread out the prepared vegetable chunks on the sheet. Add the vinegar and oil to the vegetables and toss well, using your hands and making sure all the vegetables are well coated. Lightly sprinkle salt and pepper over the entire sheet of vegetables. Bake on the center oven rack for about 12 to 15 minutes. Outer edges of the vegetables should become nice and toasted, even slightly burned, but watch closely so as not to go overboard.

Makes 8 servings

Sweet Sesame Green Beans

TAMAI FAMILY FARM

1 pound washed and trimmed whole, stringless green beans (remove the stem end only; the tail end is very tender)
3 teaspoons sugar
2 teaspoons soy sauce
¼ teaspoon sesame seed oil
¼ teaspoon toasted sesame seeds

Bring a large pot of water to a rapid boil and blanch the green beans for 2 to 3 minutes—until crisp yet tender. Remove immediately from the heat and strain. Quickly place the beans in ice water to prevent further cooking. Once they've cooled, strain the beans and set aside.

In a small saucepan over low heat, add the sugar and soy sauce, and heat just until the sugar has melted. Add the oil and sesame seeds and remove from the heat.

Coat the bottom of a frying pan or wok with vegetable oil. When the oil becomes hot, quickly add the strained green beans, along with the sauce mixture. Toss the beans in the mixture until all the beans are nicely coated and heated through.

Makes 4 servings

Battered Fried Zucchini

J&P ORGANICS

2 tablespoons sunflower oil
1 zucchini, cut in ¼" rounds
1 cup instant pancake batter, mixed according to the proportions in the package instructions, using milk in place of water*
¾ cup milk
Salt and freshly ground pepper to taste
* Florencia uses Aunt Jemima pancake mix.

Pour the sunflower oil into a skillet and put onto a low flame. Dip the zucchini rounds in the batter until completely covered and place the battered slices into the oil, making sure not to crowd them. Fry until golden brown, turning once with tongs to ensure that the rounds are golden on each side. Sprinkle with salt and freshly ground pepper when the slices are still hot. Enjoy immediately.

Makes 4 servings

Oven-Roasted Zucchini

WINDBORNE FARM

This flavorful dish brings out the best flavor in zucchini by slowly roasting the vegetable and reducing the amount of water in it. Any type of zucchini works well in this recipe—the classic dark green type, the slightly gray variety, or the bright yellow variety.

8 zucchini
6 tablespoons olive oil
1 teaspoon salt
2 or 3 sprigs fresh basil

Preheat the oven to 375°F. After trimming off and discarding the ends, cut the zucchini in half, and then into ½" slices. Lay the chunks of zucchini in a shallow ovenproof dish large enough to hold them in a double layer—a large cast-iron skillet works well, as does a ceramic lasagna pan. Toss them gently with the oil and sprinkle with the salt. Roast the zucchini until they are shriveled and browned, turning once or twice during roasting. Fully cooking them will require at least 30 minutes in the hot oven or up to 45 minutes, depending on how fresh they are. After the zucchini have roasted, let them cool at room temperature for at least 30 minutes, and sprinkle with fresh basil leaves before serving.

Makes 6 to 8 servings

Kale Ceviche

TIERRA MIGUEL FARM

4 stalks kale, stems removed and leaves chopped into medium shreds
2 scallions, roots removed and the white sections chopped
1 watermelon radish, peeled, thinly sliced, and quartered
2 carrots, peeled and thinly sliced
Juice of 1 lemon
1 tablespoon olive oil
Soy sauce to taste
Freshly ground pepper to taste

Mix together all the ingredients and serve. You can use any colorful combination of vegetables in addition to or instead of the kale, including exotic and robust dark greens such as mizuna, Chinese cabbage, baby beets, and baby turnip greens. This salad gets more delicious if left to marinate for 10 to 15 minutes.

Makes 4 servings

Marcy's Peach
Nectarine Sa

MASUMOTO FARM

1 large (or 2 medium) yell
diced
2 medium nectarines, d
½ bunch fresh cilantr
½ red bell pepper, dic
½ red onion, diced (
may be substitut
1 jalapeño pepper,
Juice of 1 lime
Salt, freshly gro
to taste

Gently toss th
pepper, onior
lime juice ar
and chili p
30 minute
Chile Rel
grilled c
other g

Or, i
add
a b
m

Eggplant Curry Soup

VANG FAMILY FARM

Chinese and Japanese eggplant are different, though both are slender and thin-skinned. Some say Japanese eggplant has a more bitter taste. Bamboo shoots are available fresh in northern California and the Northwest; look online for information on soaking and preparing the fresh shoots. Canned shoots also work well in this recipe.

2 or 3 Chinese eggplant, thinly sliced
1 tablespoon yellow curry paste (available in specialty food shops)
1 can coconut milk
¾ cup sliced bamboo shoots
¾ pound chicken breast and thigh, cubed into ½" pieces
3 or 4 lemon tree leaves (optional; 1 stalk lemongrass can be substituted)
Salt to taste

Place all the ingredients in a medium saucepan and add cold water to cover. Bring the mixture to a low boil, then simmer until the chicken is cooked to your preference. Add salt to taste. This thick stew can be served over rice.

Makes 4 servings

Homemade Whole Wheat Pasta

SLOW FOOD NATION KITCHEN

These fresh, flavorful noodles are the perfect companion to the full-flavored Cilantro Pesto.

3 cups whole wheat flour
1 cup all-purpose flour
1 teaspoon salt
5 eggs
2 tablespoons olive oil

Mix the 2 flours and the salt in a bowl and turn onto a wooden pastry board. Make a well in the center of the flour. Mix the eggs, breaking the yolks with a fork. Add the olive oil and pour the egg mixture into the well. Using a fork, mix the flour from the sides of the well into the egg-and-oil mixture. When the mixture becomes too stiff to work with a fork, continue forming the dough with your hands. Shape the dough into a ball and turn it onto the countertop. At this point, the dough should be firm enough to handle, but soft and elastic. Mix in a little extra flour if the mixture sticks to your hands. Using the base of your palms, flatten the dough ball and knead it from the middle outward. Knead both sides, keeping the ball round, until the dough's consistency is even and elastic (about 15 minutes of kneading—this stage can also be done in a mixer with a dough hook). Let the dough rest for an hour.

Divide the dough into four equal pieces and knead briefly again. Take one ball of dough at a time, flatten it with your hand or a rolling pin, and run it through the thickest setting on a pasta machine. Start reducing the settings, sprinkling extra flour on the dough each time you run it through. When the sheet of dough is $\frac{1}{8}$" to $\frac{1}{16}$" thick, cut it with a knife or pizza cutter into strips about $\frac{1}{2}$" wide. As you work, pile the fresh noodles on a plate, keeping the layers of pasta from sticking together by dusting them with flour.

Makes 4 servings

Cilantro Pesto

REDWOOD ROOTS FARM

Lighter than a rich basil pesto, this blend of fresh cilantro and spicy garlic makes a zesty condiment for any number of dishes. It is also exceptional as an appetizer spread.

1 cup lightly packed cilantro, trimmed and washed
¼ cup vinegar (rice, white, or wine)
1 tablespoon sugar or honey
2 to 4 cloves garlic
¼ to ½ cup toasted sunflower seeds or walnuts, finely chopped
1 medium-size hot red chile pepper or ¼ teaspoon powdered cayenne pepper
½ teaspoon salt

Finely chop the cilantro by hand or in a food processor. Mix together the vinegar, sugar, garlic, seeds or nuts, and chile pepper, and chop this mixture finely or process to a coarse paste. Blend the cilantro and nut paste together. Mix in the salt. Let the pesto sit for at least an hour. If desired, add more sugar, vinegar, and chile to taste. The pesto should be tangy, slightly sweet, and just a tad spicy.

Makes 4 servings

Tomato Sauce from Fresh Tomatoes

SLOW FOOD NATION KITCHEN

This bright, flavorful sauce is perfect in the heat of summer, when tomatoes are abundant.

3 large tomatoes
6 tablespoons olive oil
2 cloves garlic, minced
1 teaspoon salt
1 bunch fresh herbs (optional)

Grate the tomatoes on a box grater. This will remove the skins and seeds, leaving a soft pulp. Heat the olive oil in a large skillet. Add the garlic and cook on low heat for 3 minutes. Add the grated tomato pulp and cook until reduced by about one-third—approximately 20 minutes. Add the salt and, if you like, a handful of fresh herbs. Serve on pasta al dente (spaghetti and tagliatelle both work well) with a generous topping of grated Parmesan.

Makes 4 servings

Grilled Tilapia

MOUA FAMILY FARM

The Mouas' Herb Sauce for Fish goes well with widemouthed bass, tilapia, and mackerel. Here's a simple recipe for tilapia, one of many fish recipes that will work with the sauce.

Brush a grill rack with oil and heat the grill to medium-high. Grill a whole, gutted tilapia until it's just opaque in the center, 3 to 5 minutes per side. Serve hot, covered in the herb sauce.

Serves 4 to 6, depending on size of fish

Herb Sauce for Fish

MOUA FAMILY FARM

5 medium-size chile peppers
20 sprigs cilantro
5 sprigs dill
1 bunch basil (Italian—not Thai—basil is preferable for this recipe)
12 cherry tomatoes, quartered
2 tablespoons olive oil
1 teaspoon fish sauce
2 teaspoons soy sauce
2 teaspoons water
Salt to taste

Chop the chile peppers, cilantro, dill, and basil together with a large chef's knife until they are a fine paste. Add the olive oil, fish sauce, soy sauce, quartered tomatoes, and water to the paste. Pour over the fish after it's cooked, salt to taste, and serve.

Makes 1½ cups

Chicken and Chile Leaves

MOUA FAMILY FARM

2 whole chicken breasts, deboned and diced into 1" cubes
4 tablespoons olive oil
1 bunch chile pepper leaves (leave the flowers and young chile peppers attached to the leaves)
Salt
2 teaspoons water

Cook the chicken in half of the olive oil over high heat until slightly browned. Rinse the chile pepper leaves, lightly shred them, and toss them in another stir-fry pan with the remaining olive oil. The Moua family recommends coating the leaves in the oil—this makes them retain flavor and cook more evenly. Add the chicken to the second pan and toss the mixture over high heat for about 1 minute. Turn off the heat. Mix salt to taste into the water, then add the salty water to the dish, and serve.

Makes 4 servings

Dutch-Oven Pot Roast with Root Vegetables

BURROUGHS FAMILY FARM

The Burroughses use organic grass-fed beef from their own herd.

3 pounds rump roast, chuck roast, or other cut suitable for pot roast
2 tablespoons butter
2 tablespoons extra-virgin olive oil
Onions, garlic, and mushrooms to taste
2 cups beef stock or other liquid, such as wine, juice, or water
1 dozen small red potatoes
1 pound carrots, peeled and cut into sticks (or substitute coarsely chopped turnips or parsnips)
Generous dollop sour cream (or substitute 2 tablespoons arrowroot mixed with 2 tablespoons water)
Sea salt and freshly ground pepper to taste

In a large cast-iron skillet or Dutch oven, slowly brown the meat on all sides, using the butter and olive oil. Remove the roast and caramelize the onions, garlic, and mushrooms in the skillet. Pour off and discard the drippings and season with sea salt and freshly ground pepper to taste. Put the roast back in the pot and add the beef stock or other liquid. Cover the pan with a tight-fitting lid to contain the steam and simmer on the stovetop or in the oven (at 300°F) until fork tender—about 3 hours.

While it's simmering, check the pot periodically to ensure that the liquid hasn't completely evaporated. If it has, add more liquid. It's okay to use water, although liquid other than water will add more flavor to your broth. Add the potatoes and carrots or other root vegetables during the last hour of simmering.

To make sauce, remove the meat and vegetables to a platter, add the sour cream to the pot, and bring to a boil on the stove. Or add a spoonful at a time of arrowroot mixture until the desired thickness is obtained. Season with salt and pepper to taste.

Keep the beef covered and wait 10 to 15 minutes. Letting the beef stand gives the natural juices time to redistribute and reduces moisture loss. Pour the sauce over the meat and vegetables. Carve the meat into slices by cutting across the grain.

Makes 8 servings

Aida Brenneis's Chile Relleno Casserole

PIXIE GROWERS

Jim says the chile peppers can be prepared a couple of days ahead, and the tomato sauce can also be prepared ahead of time. The batter must be prepared at the last minute.

12 to 16 fresh poblano or pasilla chile peppers
1 large white onion, coarsely chopped
1 tablespoon olive oil
1 can (28 ounces) crushed tomatoes
½ teaspoon cinnamon, preferably freshly
  ground *canela*
1 teaspoon black pepper
2 cups chicken broth
6 eggs
2 tablespoons flour
½ teaspoon salt
3 cups grated Monterey Jack cheese or *queso
  fresco*

Blacken the chile peppers under the broiler or on a gas burner, turning until all sides are done. Put them in a paper bag or a closed glass container for 10 minutes to facilitate peeling. Remove from the container and take off the skin, halve the peppers, and remove the seeds and stems.

In a skillet, brown the onion in the oil. Puree the tomatoes in a blender and add to the onion, along with the cinnamon and black pepper. Cook over medium-high heat, stirring regularly, until the mixture comes to a boil. Boil briskly to reduce until it becomes thick, about 25 minutes. Stir in the chicken broth. Partially cover the skillet, reduce the heat, and simmer for another 45 minutes or so.

Preheat the oven to 350°F. Separate the egg yolks from the whites. Beat the whites till they hold soft peaks, then beat in the yolks 2 at a time. Finally, beat in the flour and salt. Lightly grease a baking dish with olive oil. Layer the egg batter, grated cheese, and peppers in the dish, starting with egg batter, then the cheese, then the chile peppers, and repeat, ending with a layer of batter. Place in the oven and bake until the top is well browned. With a spatula, pull the contents away from the edge of the baking dish, pour the tomato broth over the top, and serve.

Makes 12 servings

Braised Chard with Pulled Pork

J&P ORGANICS

Florencia uses meat from pork ribs for this recipe; other flavorful cuts with slight marbling work equally well.

1 teaspoon salt, plus additional salt to taste
½ pound cubed pork, chopped into rectangular pieces about 4" long, 2" wide, and 2" deep*
1 bunch chard (about 20 stalks)
⅓ cup roughly chopped white or red onions
1 small tomato
¼ cup olive oil
* The grain of the pork should run the length of the pieces, not the width—this will make the meat easy to pull apart after cooking.

In a medium-size saucepan, bring 8 cups of water to 170°F. (You can use a roasting thermometer or a candy thermometer to measure the temperature.) Add salt to the water, then add the pork, and cook the pork for 25 minutes. Keep checking the temperature to make sure it does not exceed 170°F—it should remain constant at that temperature throughout cooking. Strain the pork, saving the cooking liquid if you like for a broth base. Let the pork pieces cool slightly and pull each piece into four pieces with your hands. (You should be able to tear it along the meat's natural grain.)

While the pork is cooking, wash the chard stems under cold running water. Pull the green leaves off the red stems and chop the stems into 1" lengths. Tear each of the leaves into a few large pieces. Pour 2 cups water into a 10" saucepan, heat to boiling, add the chard stems, and cook, covered, until tender. Add the leaves to the pot, cover, and cook for 1 more minute. Pour the olive oil into a skillet, heat, and add the onion and tomato. Cook for 5 minutes over medium heat, stirring frequently with a wooden spoon. Add the pulled pork and chard to the tomato and onion mixture and braise at low temperature for another 5 minutes. Take off the heat and add salt to taste.

Makes 4 servings

California Cloverleaf Farms Organic Cheesecake

BURROUGHS FAMILY FARM

Meredith makes this cake with Organic Valley dairy and eggs.

FOR THE CRUST:
6 tablespoons unsalted butter
4 tablespoons sugar
2 large egg yolks
1 cup all-purpose flour
1 cup ground roasted organic almonds
1 teaspoon baking powder
¼ teaspoon sea salt

FOR THE CHEESECAKE BATTER:
3 packages Organic Valley cream cheese, softened
¾ cup sugar
1 teaspoon lemon peel, freshly grated
1 tablespoon lemon juice
3 large eggs

FOR THE TOPPING:
1 cup sour cream
2 tablespoons sugar
1 teaspoon vanilla
Seasonal fresh fruit (optional)

Position a rack in the center of the oven and preheat the oven to 350°F. Using a mixer, beat the butter and sugar together until fluffy. Beat in the egg yolks until smooth. Combine the flour, almonds, baking powder, and salt and fold into the butter mixture. (It will be crumbly.) Place the mixture in a springform pan and, using your fingers, press the mixture up the sides of the pan and evenly around the bottom. Bake for 15 to 20 minutes, until the crust is golden and firm. Allow to cool slightly before covering with the cheesecake batter.

Using a mixer, beat the cream cheese until smooth. Slowly add the sugar and beat until combined. Add the lemon peel and juice and beat again. Scrape down the sides and, adding the eggs one at a time, beat until combined. Pour the batter into the crust in the springform pan and cook for 10 minutes at 450°F. Decrease the temperature to 300°F and cook for an additional 30 minutes. Meanwhile, whisk together the sour cream, sugar, and vanilla and pour over the batter after the cake is cooked. Return to the oven at 300°F for an additional 10 minutes. Remove and allow to cool on a wire rack. Chill for 6 to 12 hours, then top with fruit if desired.

Makes 8 servings

Peach Crostata

MASUMOTO FARM

This crostata is excellent with vanilla-bean ice cream or fresh whipped cream.

FOR THE CRUST:
1¼ cups unbleached all-purpose flour
⅓ cup sugar
¼ teaspoon salt
1 stick (8 tablespoons) unsalted butter
1 egg yolk

FOR THE FILLING:
½ cup sugar
3 tablespoons flour
5 or 6 medium peaches, peeled and sliced into
    ½" wedges
3 tablespoons peach or apricot jam (optional,
    depending on sweetness of peaches
Ground cinnamon

To make the crust, pulse the flour, sugar, salt, and butter in a food processor (or blend by hand with a pastry blender) until crumbly. Add the egg yolk and continue to pulse until evenly combined. The dough will be crumbly and quite dry. Put it into a 9" tart pan with a removable bottom and pat firmly and evenly across the bottom and up the sides.

Preheat the oven to 375°F. Combine the sugar and flour in a small bowl until well mixed, pour over the peaches, and toss gently. Arrange the peaches in a single layer on the unbaked crust in the tart pan. If the peaches are ripe and sweet, ample juices will build up. Pour the sweet juice over the peaches. If your peaches are tart and not much juice develops, heat the jam for a few seconds in the microwave oven (or over low heat on the stove) and brush the warm jam over the peaches. Sprinkle lightly with cinnamon.

Place the tart pan on a baking sheet or other pan to collect any juices that may boil over, and bake for 35 minutes, or until the crust is golden and the peach juices are bubbly. When it's done, remove the crostata from the oven and let it cool at room temperature until you're ready to serve.

Makes 6 to 8 servings

Agua Fresca de Frambuesas (Fresh Raspberry Water)

J&P ORGANICS

5 cups plus 5 tablespoons water
2 baskets (16 ounces each) raspberries
Sugar to taste

Pour the water into a blender and add the two baskets of raspberries. Blend, then pour the blend through a sieve to strain the seeds. If the liquid does not pass easily through the colander, rub the bottom of the sieve with a rubber spatula to push the liquid through. Add sugar to taste, although with good, flavorful raspberries, you won't need much sugar. Mix the raspberries and sugar with a large whisk or wooden spoon until the sugar dissolves. This *Agua Fresca* can be served at room temperature or on ice.

Makes 6 cups

Stripey Citrus Frozen Pops

PIXIE GROWERS

Lisa's recipe creates eight frozen pops of citrus fruit juice in different colors.

Juice of 3 Moro blood oranges (for magenta color)
Juice of 4 large tangerines, such as Page or Gold Nugget (for orange color)
Juice of 2 Oro Blanco pomelos (for platinum color) (This should add up to about 3 cups)

Pour the juice of one of the types of fruit into frozen-pop molds. Put the molds in the freezer for 2 hours, then add one of the remaining juices and repeat. Insert a pop stick into a partially frozen layer partway through the process. Let the pops freeze overnight.

Optional: Add a little corn syrup to sweeten the juice and to make the frozen surface shinier.

Makes 8 pops

Sautéed Peaches

MASUMOTO FARM

2 tablespoons butter
3 large, ripe, yellow-flesh peaches, sliced
½ tablespoon lemon juice
1 tablespoon brown sugar
¼ teaspoon ground cinnamon
1 tablespoon brandy or other favorite liqueur (optional)

In a skillet, melt the butter, then add the sliced peaches. Sauté the peaches over medium heat until they're heated through but not overcooked. Natural juices will form in the cooking process. Add the lemon juice, brown sugar, cinnamon, and brandy (if desired), lightly tossing until the flavorings are well blended. Serve over your favorite crepes, pancakes, waffles, or French toast. (Marcy likes Spiced Rye/Buttermilk Waffles with Pecans.) If you like, garnish with a dollop of whipped cream, mint leaves, and/or lemon peel.

Makes 3 or 4 servings

Apple Pie

SLOW FOOD NATION KITCHEN

FOR THE CRUST:
1 teaspoon salt
2 cups all-purpose flour
¾ teaspoon salt
4 or 5 tablespoons ice water

FOR THE FILLING:
5 large Gravenstein or Gala apples
¼ cup apple juice
Juice of one small lemon
½ cup brown sugar
4 tablespoons butter (room temperature)
2 tablespoons all-purpose flour
1 teaspoon cinnamon
¼ teaspoon nutmeg

To make the crust, add the salt to the flour and blend in a food processor. Add the butter and pulse on and off until the mixture resembles coarse meal. Slowly pour in 4 tablespoons of ice water into the processor, just until the dough gathers together. Remove the dough from the machine and divide it into two equal pieces. Flatten each piece with your palm to form a disk; wrap in wax paper, and chill in the refrigerator for at least 45 minutes.

Preheat the oven to 350°F. Peel and core the apples, and slice them into ⅓" slices. Combine the slices with the apple juice, lemon juice, sugar, butter, flour, cinnamon, and nutmeg in a bowl.

Remove one disk of dough from the refrigerator. Unwrap it and roll out on a lightly floured work surface to form a circle about ⅛" thick and 2" larger than the pie plate. Fold it into quarters and gently transfer it to the pie plate, placing the corner of the dough in the center of the plate. Trim the dough, leaving a 1" overhang. Repeat the rolling process for a top crust; for this one, the circle should be 1" larger than the pie plate.

Pile the apple mixture into the pie plate. Drape the second disk of piecrust over the apple filling, and pinch the edges to fasten to bottom crust. Score the top crust with two 2" long cuts. Sprinkle an extra teaspoon of sugar on the top crust if you like. Bake for 50 minutes to an hour—the top crust should be a deep golden brown when the pie is ready. Let cool for at least an hour before serving.

Makes 8 servings

Drink unbottled water.

Learn your region's food story.

Try making things from scratch.

Plant a kitchen garden.

How to

Buy organic.

Avoid genetically modified food.

Conserve, compost, and recycle.

Eat together.

About Slow Food

SLOW FOOD INTERNATIONAL

Slow Food is a nonprofit, ecogastronomic, member-supported organization that was founded in 1989 to counteract fast food and fast life; the disappearance of local food traditions and people's dwindling interest in the food they eat, where it comes from, how it tastes; and how our food choices affect the rest of the world.

Today, Slow Food has more than 100,000 members in 132 countries. For more information, visit www.slowfood.com.

SLOW FOOD USA

Slow Food USA envisions a future American food system that is based on the principles of high quality and taste, environmental sustainability, and social justice—in essence, a food system that is good, clean, and fair. The organization seeks to catalyze a broad cultural shift away from the destructive effects of an industrial food system and fast life and toward the regenerative cultural, social, and economic benefits of a sustainable food system, regional food traditions, the pleasures of the table, and a slower and more harmonious rhythm of life. For more information, visit www.slowfoodusa.org.

SLOW FOOD NATION

Slow Food Nation is a nonprofit subsidiary of Slow Food USA. It was created by Alice Waters, with support from Slow Food USA, to organize the first-ever American collaborative gathering to unite the growing sustainable food movement and introduce thousands of people to food that is good, clean, and fair. Slow Food Nation is dedicated to creating events that provide a framework for deeper environmental connection to our food and aims to inspire and empower Americans to build a food system that is sustainable, healthy, and delicious. For more information, visit www.slowfoodnation.org.

Listings of Californian farmers, farmstands, and farmers' markets, along with restaurants and grocers who buy locally

Buy Fresh, Buy Local California
www.buylocalca.org

Resource for general information on state agriculture policy

California Department of Food and Agriculture
www.cdfa.ca.gov

Updates on policy issues affecting farmers

California Farm Bureau Federation
www.cfbf.com

Information about food and farming issues in the state of California

Community Alliance with Family Farmers
www.caff.org

General resources for food security work in California

California Food and Justice Coalition
www.foodsecurity.org/california

Listings of farmers, markets, and more in California and beyond

Eat Well Guide
www.eatwellguide.org

Listings of farmers, markets, and more in California and beyond

Local Harvest
www.localharvest.org

Information about advocacy and organizing for a more sustainable food system

Roots of Change
www.rocfund.org

Index

Underscored page references indicate sidebars. **Boldface** references indicate photographs.

A

African American Farmers of California, 45
African American farms, 42, 45
Almond orchards, of Burroughs Family Farms, 29, 37
Apple Pie, 153
Apricot Jam, Fast Refrigerator, 77
Ark of Taste, x, 83
Artichokes, Spearmint-Stuffed, 114, **115**
Artisan recipes, 77
Asparagus, Oven-Roasted, 118, **119**
Ayala, Oliver, **82**, 83

B

Bagley, Dan, 59, 60, **60**, **64**, 65
Barley
    Bean-and-Barley Stew, 129
Basil
    Herb Sauce for Fish, 134, **135**
Beans
    Bean-and-Barley Stew, 129
    dried, preparing, 11
    Romano, 27
Beatty, Amanda, 94
Biscuits
    Paul's Best Biscuit Recipe, 108
    Whole Wheat Biscuits, 108
Black-eyed peas
    Fresh Black-Eyed Peas, 117
    of Will Scott Jr., 42
Brait, Andrew, 3
Brait, Anna, 3
Breads
    Whole Wheat Flat Bread, 110, **111**
    of Windborne CSA, 49
Brenneis, Lisa, 79, 81, 83
Burroughs, Benina, 37
Burroughs, Bruce, 29
Burroughs, Meredith, 37
Burroughs, Rosie, 29, 33, **36**, 37
Burroughs, Ward, 29, 33, **36**, 37
Burroughs, Zeb, 37

Burroughs Family Farms, 28–37
    recipes of, 108, 142, 146
Buttermilk Dressing, 118
Buxman, Paul, **12**, 13, 16, 19
Buxman, Pauline, **14**, 19
Buxman, Ruth, 13, 16, 19
Buxman, Wyeth, 16, **17**, 19
Bylsma, Brian, 37
Bylsma, Christina, 33, 37
Bylsma, Jed, **28**

C

California Clean, 16
California Farmland Conservancy Program (CFCP), 104, 105
Cast-iron pot, 91
Cattle
    at Burroughs Family Farms, 29, **30–31**, 33
    at Clark Summit Farm, 59, 60, **64**, 65
CFCP, 104, 105
Chard
    Braised Chard with Pulled Pork, 144, **145**
    of J&P Organics, 85
Cheese, Yogurt, 77
Cheesecake, California Cloverleaf Farms Organic, 146, **147**
Chicken coops, at Burroughs Family Farms, **35**, 37
Chicken(s)
    Chicken and Chile Leaves, 138, **139**
    at Clark Summit Farm, 60, **61**, **62–63**, 65
    Simple Roast Chicken, 140, **141**
Chickpea Puree, Jennifer's, 116
Chile Leaves, Chicken and, 138, **139**
Chile peppers
    Aida Brenneis's Chile Relleno Casserole, 143
    Chile Relleno Bake, 136
    Herb Sauce for Fish, 134, **135**

Churchill, Jim, 79, **80**, 81, 83
Cilantro
    Cilantro Pesto, 133
    Herb Sauce for Fish, 134, **135**
Clark Summit Farm, **xiv**, 58–65
    recipe of, 140
Coalition with Family Farmers, 4
Collins, Mirabai, **99**
Community Farm of Ann Arbor, 99
Community Supported Agriculture (CSA), xiii, 4, 9, 49, 52, 57, 65, 93–99, 104, 105
Cooking from scratch, benefits of, 11
Corn on the Cob Recipe, The Truth About, 116
CSA. *See* Community Supported Agriculture
Cucumber Salad, 126, **127**
Cunninghame, Liz, 59, 60, **60**, 65
Czarnecki, Janet, 93, 94, **95**, 99

D

Dairies
    of Burroughs Family Farms, 29, 33, 37
    industrial, 29, 33, 59
Derden-Little, Erin, 94
Desem starter, for bread, 110
Devers, Chris, 105
Dill
    Herb Sauce for Fish, 134, **135**

E

Ecology, balanced, signs of, 13, 16
Eggplant
    Eggplant Curry Soup, 130, **131**
    Pastaless Vegetable Lasagna, 128

F

Factory farming, xiii
Family farming, decline of, 23–24

Farmer, expanded definition of, 9
Farmers' markets, ix, 41–42, 45, 65, 70, 75, 83, 99
Farms. *See also specific names*
    arguments for saving, 101
    disappearance of, 101
    locations of, **xiv–xv**
    teachings from, ix
Fava Bean Salad, Warm, 112
Food dehydrator, 11, 91
Food storage techniques, 11
Friend's Ranches, 79, **80**, 81, 83
Frozen Pops, 77
    Stripey Citrus Frozen Pops, 150
Fujimoto, Bill, x, 83
Full Belly Farm, **xiv**, 2–9, 52
    recipes of, 112, 114, 118, 140
Full Circle Dairy, **xiv**, 33, 37. *See also* Burroughs Family Farms

G

Garlic, China Rose, **96–97**
Grains, of Windborne Farm, 49, 52, 57
Green Beans, Sweet Sesame, 122
Greene, Jennifer, **48**, 49, 52, **55**, 57, 110
Green kitchen tools, 91
Greens, Stewed, 117

H

Heirloom varieties, x, 27
Herb pot, 91
Herbs
    dried, uses for, 11
    Herb Sauce for Fish, 134, **135**
Honey and Nuts, 77

J

J&P Organics, **xv**, 84–89
    recipes of, 122, 144, 150
Jujube, 75

K

Kale Ceviche, 124
Krecu, Milijan, **102**, 105

L

Land conservation, by Tierra Miguel Farm, 102–5
Laotian Hmong farmers, 67–75
Lasagna, Pastaless Vegetable, 128
Leased land, 70, 89
Legumes. *See also* Beans
 of Windborne Farm, 49, 52
Levendoski, Beth Ann, 104, 105
Live Power Community Farm, 52

M

Masumoto, Korio, ix, **xi**
Masumoto, Marcy, ix, **xi**, xiii
Masumoto, Mas, **viii**, ix–x, **xi**, **xii**, xiii
Masumoto, Nikiko, ix, **xi**
Masumoto Farm, **xv**
 recipes of, 126, 136, 148, 152
Meat producer, Clark Summit Farm as, 58–65
Menu planning, based on fresh ingredients, ix
Mexican squash
 Medley of Roasted Vegetables with Balsamic Vinegar, 120
Milk
 from Burroughs Family Farms, 29, **32**, 37
 raw vs. pasteurized, 39
Monocultural farms, 86, 89
Monterey Market, 83
Mortar and pestle, 91
Moua, Michael, 70, **74**
Moua, Va, **66**, 70, 75
Moua Family Farm, **xv**, 70–75
 recipes of, 134, 138
Muller, Paul, 3, 4, 9

N

National Organic Program, 47
Nectarines
 Marcy's Peach & Nectarine Salsa, 126
 of Masumoto Farm, x
 of Sweet Home Ranch, **18**
Nuts, Honey and, 77

O

Ojai Pixie Growers Association, 78–83
Onions
 Pastaless Vegetable Lasagna, 128

Oranges
 Stripey Citrus Frozen Pops, 150
Organic certification, 16, 19, 47
Organic farming
 at Burroughs Family Farms, 29, 37
 at Full Belly Farm, 3, 4
 at J&P Organics, 84–89
 at Sweet Home Ranch, 13, 16
 of Will Scott Jr., 41, 42
Organic Valley, 33

P

Pasta, Homemade Whole Wheat, 132
Pasteurization of milk, 39
Pauma Band of Mission Indians, 103, 105
Peaches
 Marcy's Peach & Nectarine Salsa, 126
 of Masumoto Farm, ix, x, **xii**, xiii
 Peach Crostata, 148
 Sautéed Peaches, 152
Peppers, bell
 Medley of Roasted Vegetables with Balsamic Vinegar, 120
Perez, Florencia, 86, 89
Perez, Juan, 84, 85, 86, 89
Perez, Pablo, **84**, 85, 86, **88**, 89
Pesto, Cilantro, 133
Pickles, Refrigerator, 77
Pigs
 at Clark Summit Farm, **58**, 60, **64**, 65
 Suckling Pig, 140
Pixie Growers, **xv**, 78–83
 recipes of, 143, 150
Pomelos
 Stripey Citrus Frozen Pops, 150
Pork
 Braised Chard with Pulled Pork, 144, **145**
 Suckling Pig, 140
Pot Roast, Dutch-Oven, with Root Vegetables, 142
Preserves
 how to make, 21
 Sweet Home Ranch, **15**, 19
Pumpkin Leaf Soup, Sweet, 136

R

Raspberries
 Agua Fresca de Frambuesas (Fresh Raspberry Water), 150, **151**
Redmond, Judith, **2**, 3, 4, **6**, 9, 112, 114
Redwood Roots Farm, **xiv**, 92–99
 recipes of, 129, 133
Rivers, Dru, 3
Root Vegetables, Dutch-Oven Pot Roast with, 142

S

Safeway organic foods, 47
Salad dressings
 Buttermilk Dressing, 118
 Judith's Salad Dressing, 112
Scott, Will, Jr., **xv**, **40**, 41–45
 recipe of, 117
Shiva, Vandana, ix
Slow food
 definition of, v
 how to practice, **154–55**
Slow Food International, 157
Slow Food Nation, 157
Slow Food Nation Kitchen, recipes of, 117, 132, 133, 153
Slow Food USA, 157
Strawberries, of Tamai Family Farms, 23, 24
Subsistence farming, 67
Sustainability, xiii, 3, 4, 19, 45, 59, 60, 93, 94, **101**, 104
Sweet Home Ranch, **xv**, 12–19
 recipe of, 108

T

Tamai, Aaron, **22**, 24
Tamai, Daisy, 120
Tamai, Gloria, 23, 24, **25**
Tamai, Jason, **22**, 23, 24, 27
Tamai, Julia, **22**, 24, 27
Tamai, Steve, 24, **25**
Tamai Family Farms, **xv**, 22–27
 recipes of, 116, 120, 122
Tangerines
 Pixie, **78**, 79–83
 Stripey Citrus Frozen Pops, 150
Tanner, Eddie, 99

Terra-cotta crock, 91
Thacher, Anne, 81
Thacher, Emily, 79, 81, 83
Thacher, Tony, 79, 81
Thao, Xia, 67, **68**
Tierra Miguel Farm, **xv**, 102–5
 recipes of, 118, 124, 128
Tierra Miguel Foundation, 104, 105
Tilapia, Grilled, 134
Tomatoes, fresh
 Pastaless Vegetable Lasagna, 128
 for sauce, 11
 saving, 11
 of Tamai Family Farms, 24, 27
 Tomato Sauce from Fresh Tomatoes, 133
Tools, for green kitchen, 91
Tree adoption, xiii

U

USDA Organic seal, 47

V

Vang, Chao, 67, **69**, 70
Vang Family Farm, **xv**, 67–70, 126
 recipes of, 130, **131**, 136

W

Waters, Alice, **viii**, ix, x, xiii, 157
West Oakland Farmers' Market, 41–42, 45
Windborne Farm, **xiv**, 48–57
 recipes of, 110, **111**, 116, 124

Y

Yogurt Cheese, 77

Z

Zucchini
 Battered Fried Zucchini, 122, **123**
 Medley of Roasted Vegetables with Balsamic Vinegar, 120
 Oven-Roasted Zucchini, 124, **125**
 Pastaless Vegetable Lasagna, 128

CONTRIBUTORS

Anya Fernald, the executive director of Slow Food Nation, spent a year after college documenting traditional cheesemaking in Tunisia, Greece, Italy, and other Mediterranean locales, and her life has really never been the same. A passion for farms and farming that was ignited on dairy farms led her to Slow Food International, where she worked for five years as program director of the Slow Food Foundation. She went on to run the Buy Fresh, Buy Local campaign and other advocacy initiatives as program director of the California-based Community Alliance with Family Farmers. Anya lobbied for *Come to the Table* to be dedicated entirely to cheese, but her pleas were ignored. She helped develop the idea for the book and added her expertise to the recipes.

Katrina Heron is a writer and editor and chair of the board of Slow Food Nation. She and her twin daughters are regulars at the Berkeley Tuesday Farmers' Market, where Full Belly Farm has a stall.

Nathanael Johnson is a freelance journalist in San Francisco. He has contributed to National Public Radio, *This American Life*, *Outside*, and *Harper's Magazine*. He is two generations away from farming: His grandfather moved off the farm to work in food policy but apparently the urge has not cleared from the blood. He often writes about agriculture.

Carol Ness, a San Francisco Bay Area writer and farmer groupie, has tasted irradiated strawberries, counted fruits and vegetables at three Whole Foods Markets to see how many were locally grown, and donned a white paper bunny suit to range freely inside an egg producer's chicken coop — all in the interest of connecting people with the realities of their food supply. Her recent work on sustainable food has appeared mainly in the *San Francisco Chronicle*.

PHOTOGRAPHERS

Aya Brackett was born and raised in a traditional Japanese house in the mountains of Northern California. She grew up with two wood stoves, a generator for electricity, and a long dirt road. She spent four years as a photo editor at *Dwell* magazine, where she contributed her own photography and styled food and props for many shoots. Her love of food and design informs her photography and fuels a constant search for the unusual and inspiring.

Emily Nathan is a Bay Area photographer whose work has appeared in *Gourmet*, *Real Simple*, *Conde Nast Traveler*, *Make*, and *Dwell*.

Jenny Elia Pfeiffer is an Oakland-based artist and photographer. Her portraits and travel photography have appeared in several local and national publications, including *ReadyMade*, *Sunset*, *Budget Travel*, *San Francisco Magazine*, and *InStyle*. She also collaborates with her sister Lisa Pfeiffer on multimedia works that have been featured in galleries in San Francisco and Prague. Jenny and her husband just started receiving a veggie box from Full Belly Farm once a week and have both become big fans of kale.

Alexander Stock is a recreational photographer who found he made a lot of new friends when he carried a crate of strawberries through security and onto the plane on the way home from Tamai Family Farms.

Kim Westerman is the senior editor at *Pulse Guides* (www.pulseguides.com), as well as a freelance writer and photographer based in Berkeley, California.

DESIGNERS

David Albertson runs a design agency in San Francisco and has created the advertising and brand identity for Slow Food Nation. His team is responsible for the selection of images, typographic styling, and illustration throughout this book. Contributors from his office were Kirk von Rohr and Jay Roop.

Special Thanks: Sylvan Brackett, Vera Ciametti, Jen Dalton, Talia Dillman, Carolyn Federman, Gordon Jenkins, Paige Lansing, Sarah Weiner